Instruction in Faith (1537)

by John Calvin

Translated and Edited
by Paul T. Fuhrmann

Foreword by John H. Leith

Westminster/John Knox Press
Louisville, Kentucky

Book design by Ken Taylor

Published by Westminster/John Knox Press
Louisville, Kentucky

This book is printed on acid-free paper that meets the American
National Standards Institute Z39.48 standard. ∞

PRINTED IN THE UNITED STATES OF AMERICA
9   8   7   6   5   4   3   2   1

Library of Congress Cataloging-in-Publication Data

Calvin, Jean, 1509–1564.
   [Instruction et confession de foy. English]
   Instruction in faith (1537) / by John Calvin ; translated and
edited by Paul T. Fuhrmann ; foreword by John H. Leith.
         p.   cm.
   Translation of: Instruction et confession de foy.
   Originally published: Philadelphia : Westminster Press, 1949.
With new introd.
   Includes bibliographical references.
   ISBN 0-664-25314-8

   1. Theology, Doctrinal—Popular works—Early works to
1800. 2. Reformed Church—Doctrines—Early works to
1800.   I. Fuhrmann, Paul T.   II. Title.
BT70.C25 1992
238'.42—dc20   91-37539

Uxori Optimae
Esther
Filioque Dilecto
Joseph
Pater Familias
Interpres
D.D.D.

"La pensée fondamentale de Calvin c'est la gloire du Dieu révélé dans la Bible . . . La gloire qu'il faut rendre à Dieu c'est le croire sur parole et lui obéir par confiance."

—G. FULLIQUET

Contents

Foreword to the 1992 Edition

In August, 1536, John Calvin, journeying through Geneva, was persuaded by William Farel to remain there and participate in the reformation of the city. The city had declared on May 21, 1536, to live henceforth according to the law of the gospel and the word of God, and to abolish all papal abuses.[1] The old structures had been abolished. Now a new form and shape had to be given to the life of the church. To this end Calvin presented to the city council "Articles Concerning the Organization of the Church and of Worship at Geneva proposed by the Ministers at the Council, January 16, 1537."[2]

These articles, written by Calvin and Farel, proposed the frequent celebration of the Holy Supper, the establishment of the discipline of excommunication, provision for the singing of psalms "so that the hearts of all may be aroused and encited to make like prayers and render like praises and thanks to God with one accord." The third provision was for Christian instruction. As a consequence, the articles called for a confession of faith and also for a catechism. "The order which we advise being set up is that there be a brief and simple summary of the Christian faith, to be taught to all children, and that at certain seasons of the year they come before the ministers to be interrogated and examined, and to receive more ample explanation, according as there is need to the capacity of each one of them, until they have been proved sufficiently instructed."

Calvin's catechism of 1537, written according to the recommendation of the Ordinances, was translated by Paul T. Fuhrmann and first printed in 1949 by Westminster Press.

The catechism stands in a long tradition of Christian instruction.[3] The form Calvin gives to his catechism in 1537 is brief expositions of thirty-three heads of doctrine. In his catechism of 1542 Fr., 1545 L., Calvin adopted the question and answer method, which not only provides succinct statements of Christian faith but also helps the student to formulate the right questions.[4] This catechism replaced the *Instruction in Faith* of 1537. Yet the *Instruction in Faith* of 1537 has its own intrinsic merit, as a brief and concise summary of Calvin's early theology that he had already written in the *Institutes* of 1536.

Calvin would at the end of his life express regret that he had not had time to revise his 1542 catechism.[5] However, the need for revision was modified by the availability of a number of catechisms during Calvin's ministry in Geneva. Rodolphe Peter has identified nine catechisms, three of which predate Calvin's entrance into Geneva.[6] These catechisms were published as primers for instruction in numbers and reading as well as in the faith. Some included instruction on grammar, accents, and punctuation in addition to the ABCs and numbers. The catechisms and the primers concentrated on the Lord's Prayer, the Apostles' Creed, and the Law (the Ten Commandments). They frequently included Bible verses that were useful for facing the challenges of Christian living, and prayers for various times during the day. Calvin's own catechism of 1542 was published with prayers for use on rising, on sitting down and getting up from the table, on going to work or school, and on going to bed at night.

The primers also included simple questions and answers designed to be asked on admission to the Lord's Table. The larger catechisms were used for instruction and the more precise and simple questions were the confession for admission to the Lord's Table. A set of questions for admission to the Lord's Table was also attached to some editions of Calvin's catechism. These questions are generally very simple, for example:

Q. In whom do you believe?

A. In God the Father, and in Jesus Christ his Son, and in the Holy Spirit.

Q. The Father, the Son, and the Holy Spirit, are they more than one God?

A. No.

Q. Should we serve God according to his commandments or according to human traditions?

A. We should serve according to his commandments and not according to human commandments.

Q. Are you able to accomplish the commandments of God by yourself?

A. No.

Q. Who then accomplishes them in you?

A. The Holy Spirit.

Q. And to whom do you pray?

A. God.

Q. In whose name do you pray?

A. In the name of our Lord Jesus Christ who is our advocate and intercessor.

Q. How many sacraments are there in the Christian church?

A. Two.

Q. What are they?

A. Baptism and the Lord's Supper.

Calvin gave a high place to instruction in Christian faith. In the *Institutes of the Christian Religion*, he advocated a catechizing "in which children and those near adolescence would give account of their faith before the church. But the best method of catechizing would be to have a manual drafted for this exercise, containing and summarizing in simple manner most of the articles of our religion, on which the whole believer's church ought to agree without controversy. A child of ten would present himself to the church to declare his confession of faith, would be examined in each article and answer to each; if he were ignorant of anything or insufficiently understood it, he would be taught. Thus while the church looks on as a witness, he would profess the one, true and sincere faith, in which the believing folk with one mind worship the one God.

"If this discipline were in effect today, it would certainly arouse some slothful parents, who callously neglect the instruction of their children as a matter of no concern to them; for then they could not overlook it without public disgrace."[7]

In another place, Calvin writes, "Those to whom God has given the honor of having children, let them know that they are all the more obligated to take pains that their children are duly instructed. Thus if they wish to have good instruction, it is always necessary to begin with faith. For children could give the appearance of having all the virtue in the world, but that would be worth nothing, unless God be feared and honored by them. How frequently we see those who take great pains that their children be indoctrinated in the business of the world! It is true that they provide excellent teachers for their children, but for the purpose of making a grand show, so that they might know some three words of Latin and be able to display at the dinner table that they converse easily and can put up a good front according to the world. Yet it is never a question of knowing God! It is the wrong way to proceed! It is putting the cart before the horse."[8]

The education of a child, Calvin believed, is critically important for growth to human maturity. "When a person is poorly taught from childhood, even though he works life-long to forget the corruptions with which he has been filled, he never comes to the point that he does not retain some spot and some soil. Thus we see what grace God gives to those who are taught well."[9]

Readers of this reprinting of the *Instruction in Faith* need to remember that the Historical Foreword and the Notes, which reflect the translator's interests and concerns, were written over forty years ago and at a time when the translator probably did not have access to many Calvin studies. Hence, the Foreword and the Notes should be supplemented by more recent scholarship. The *Opera Selecta*, as well as the work of Ford Lewis Battles on the young Calvin, apparently was not available to Professor Fuhrmann.

Many students of Calvin would dispute the emphasis Professor Fuhrmann placed upon the *Instruction in Faith* as an early writing that gives the real clue to Calvin's theology. It is true that Calvin was involved in many later controversies, but some of his greatest theological writing was done at the end of his career. In addition, the early works of Calvin (1535–1541) are hardly superior because of Calvin's early character, as Fuhrmann argues. In fact, some of the harshest statements Calvin ever wrote on the doctrine of predestination are to be found in the *Institutes* of 1539.[10]

Instruction in Faith is a clear, serene, and even pleasant statement of Christian faith written by John Calvin when he was twenty-seven to twenty-eight years of age, and no more than three or four years after his mature commitment to the Christian faith. The faith to which he felt called and which ever afterward directed his life is summarized clearly and succinctly in *Instruction in Faith*. For us today it is a classic confession of a humanist scholar who was called to be a Christian and a minister in a chaotic and dangerous time. For this reason it helps us today to think and live as Christians.

JOHN H. LEITH

13

Historical Foreword

When in 1536 the fiery preacher William Farel stopped a famous wandering scholar by the name of John Calvin,[1] and persuaded him to remain and to teach the Bible in Geneva, the city was a religious and spiritual desert. In previous years the Genevese had expelled the Roman Catholic bishop and ruler of the city, but their protestantism then consisted merely in no longer attending Mass. They had freed themselves from the yoke of the bishop but were unwilling to accept the yoke of Christ. Rejecting all religious authority, they did not have the least idea of what the Christian faith might be. Their main concerns were money, business, pleasure, and sports.

The unflinching intention of Farel and Calvin, however, was to form again New Testament Christianity in Geneva, to restate it as Faith, to re-create it as Life, to re-establish it as Church. The great Jesuit theologian Cardinal Bellarmine, 1542–1621, frankly acknowledged that before the Reformers came, nothing was firm in the world: there was no severity in church courts, no discipline in morals, no erudition in sacred letters, no reverence in divine things, almost no religion.[2] That the purpose of the French Reformers was then essentially positive and constructive is clearly shown in the Declaration of the Church of France of 1559, whose Article 31 defines the Reformers as men whom God has raised in an extraordinary manner to build anew the Church which was in ruin and desolation. The French word for "to reform"[3] actually meant then "to form again." The verb "to protest" did not mean to protest against (Catholicism), but, from the Latin *protestari*, to witness, to declare publicly. Farel and Calvin were, then, reformers and protestants in

15

the original meanings of those words. They were determined to form again Christianity and to declare it publicly.

It was under these circumstances, and on Farel's suggestion, that Calvin wrote in French this *Instruction in Faith* and published it in 1537. His intention was not to gain the admiration of scholars, but to inspire a simple faith in the people of Geneva. This treatise presented to the common people the essense of his *Institutes* of 1536.[4] It is indeed Calvin's own popular compendium of his earliest *Institutio*. As this title *Instruction in Faith* suggests, this work is essentially constructive. Abstaining from debates and attacks on the Roman Church, it offers the positive tenets of the Christian faith. It aims at spiritual upbuilding and religious education. This early work of Calvin exhibits the living faith of reformed Christianity[5] in all its simplicity and grandeur. It is one of the few books that Calvin himself wrote and edited with care.[6] The strange thing is that such a stupendous statement of faith soon disappeared from circulation, was completely lost, and was buried by the later voluminous and mostly polemic productions of the Reformer. Historians knew of its existence, and wondered what the book was like. Then, three hundred and forty years after its publication, at last one original copy (printed in Gothic type and without accents) was discovered in Paris, in 1877, by H. Bordier. It was republished in Geneva in 1878, by A. Rilliet and Th. Dufour; in Germany in 1880 and 1926; in Italy in 1935; and now finally in America as the key to the understanding of the early Protestant faith in general and of Calvin in particular.

The great theological and historical importance of this *Instruction in Faith* can be readily seen. For ages, historians had sought the secret of the Reformation origins and dynamics in the old sets of the Reformers' works, but it proved impossible to go backward from the sets to the early core of Protestantism, for the very reason that such vital core, or key, was not in the older sets of Luther and Calvin. It is only the modern discovery of certain of the earliest Protestant treatises, such as Luther's 1515–1516 *Course on Romans*, Farel's 1525 *Summary*, Lambert of Avignon's 1529 *Christian Sum*, and Calvin's *Instruction in Faith*, that has allowed recent European scholarship to penetrate the inner sanctum and to possess the vital core of the Reformation. It is only in the light of such positive and constructive treatises, and when spiritually possessed by their original dynamism, that we are in a position and in a condition to know early Protestantism, to estimate properly the later work of the Reformers, and to understand the further developments of Protestant religion and theology.

This *Instruction in Faith* is of the greatest help for the understanding of Calvin himself, for it offers the early, elemental, and positive core of his religion. With this key we now can open the early Reformed sanctuary and see its simple beauty and great power. Once in possession of this *Instruction* we can, moreover, descend the course of history and understand the later works of Calvin, a thing that was impossible for our fathers. We then can realize that many of Calvin's later works are of a polemical nature, answers to all sorts of paganism and infidelity, and appreciate also the superior value of the earlier writings of the Genevese Reformer. While Calvin's later works are encumbered by long tirades and do not allow us to see clearly his early positive orientation and constructive contribution, the early works were prophetic, that is to say, inspired and inspiring, creative and positive. That was the Calvin of the early days: hopeful and constructive. There is no doubt that the early works of Calvin, 1535–1541, were superior because of Calvin's early character. In 1537 Calvin was about twenty-nine years of age—not yet old before his time; not yet opposed on all sides; not yet irritated by all kinds of misunderstandings, difficulties, cares; not yet consumed by illness. The early Calvin had a sense of Love of God, and spoke of ardent charity toward one's neighbor.

The importance of this *Instruction in Faith* should become self-evident to the reader. He will find herein the spirit of early Protestantism, which was neither a theology nor an organization, but an inspiration—the rebirth of Israel's prophetism within the Roman Catholic Church of that time. The reader will find, moreover, that the thought of this *Instruction* is clear and definite, qualities sadly needed in current Protestantism, so foggy and cold in comparison with that faith which was then an illumination of the mind and a warming of the heart.

The Bible verses at the beginning and end of this *Instruction in Faith* and the references to Bible chapters are by Calvin himself. Calvin, however, referred only to chapters, and therefore the verse numbers have been added for convenience in reference. The Scriptural quotations are everywhere John Calvin's own rendering of the original Hebrew and Greek texts. Calvin read the Bible through his own Genevese glasses. It remains to be seen, however, whether his glasses were better or worse than those of modern Bible scholars. The translator has not the least doubt that future Christian generations will decide the matter in favor of the Genevese Reformer, and will still read his Works when contemporary platitudes shall be either forgotten or derided.

Sentences in parentheses ( ) are so placed by Calvin himself, and are an integral part of this *Instruction in Faith*. Words in brackets [ ] are additions of the translator, but are, as a rule, Calvin's words taken from parallel passages of his *Institutio* of 1536 or 1539, or his *Institution* of 1541.

The use of capitals, which may appear irregular to a careful reader, is simply that of Calvin himself.

Although all the available editions of Calvin's *Opera* have been consulted in preparing this edition of the *Instruction*, the notes generally refer to the critical edition of the *Institution* of 1541, which is Calvin's translation of his *Institutio* of 1539, incorporating the first *Institutio* of 1536, edited by J. Pannier, annotated by A. Lecerf (Vol. I) and by Max Dominicé (Vols. II–IV), and republished in Paris, 1936–1939, by La Société Les Belles Lettres. This is the critical edition of Calvin's *Institution* most readily available. As there are several editions of Calvin's commentaries on Biblical books, for the convenience of the reader Calvin's expositions are referred to according to Bible book, chapter, and verse, rather than by any particular edition.

This translation is intentionally less colloquial and more exact than many common translations of French literature. It also strives to follow to the letter the form of the French text of the *Instruction in Faith* of 1537. Inasmuch as Calvin translated it into Latin "for the other churches" in 1538, however, some of Calvin's Latin renderings which either differ from the French text of 1537 or may prove to be of interest to scholars will be found in the Notes.

The translator wishes to thank Professor John T. McNeill, of the Union Theological Seminary in New York City, for encouragement, suggestions, and corrections.

PAUL T. FUHRMANN

Like children just born, desire the
reasonable milk which is without fraud.

I Peter 2:2

Be prepared to answer to each who asks
you to account for the hope which is in you.

I Peter 3:15

If a man speaks, let him speak the words
of God.

I Peter 4:11

1

All Men Are Born
in Order to Know God[7]

As no man is found, however barbarous and even savage
he may be, who is not touched by some idea[8] of religion, it is
clear that we all are created in order that we may know the
majesty of our Creator, that having known it, we may esteem
it above all and honor it with all awe,[9] love, and reverence.

But, leaving aside the unbelievers, who seek nothing
but to efface from their memory that idea[10] of God which
is planted in their hearts, we, who make profession of per-
sonal religion,[11] must reflect that this decrepit life of ours,
which will soon end, must be nothing else but a meditation
of immortality. Now, nowhere can eternal and immortal life
be found except in God. It is necessary, therefore, that the
principal care and solicitude of our life be to seek God, to
aspire to him with all the affection of our heart, and to
repose nowhere else but in him alone.

2

What Difference There Is
Between True and False Religion[12]

Since it is commonly agreed that if our life is without
religion we are most miserable and in no way better than

brute animals, no one wishes to be considered as completely alienated from piety and acknowledgment of God. There is, however, a great difference in the way[13] of declaring one's religion, because the majority of men are not truly touched by the awe of God. Yet, willingly or not, they are bound by this thought always coming anew to their minds[14] that there is some divinity by whose power they stand or fall. Hence, being astonished by the thought of such a great power, they revere it in some way in order not to provoke it against themselves by too great a contempt. Yet, living in a disorderly way and rejecting all honesty, they exhibit a great sense of security in despising the judgment of God. Moreover, they turn away from the true God because they estimate God not by his infinite majesty but by the foolish and giddy vanity of their own mind. Hence, although they may afterward strive to serve God with great care, that does not profit them at all, because they do not worship the eternal God, but the dreams and fancies of their own heart in place of God. Now the gist of true piety does not consist in a fear which would gladly flee the judgment of God but, being unable to do so, has horror of it. True piety consists rather in a pure and true zeal which loves God altogether as Father, and reveres him truly as Lord, embraces his justice and dreads to offend him more than to die. All those who possess this zeal do not undertake to forge for themselves a God as their temerity wishes, but they seek the knowledge of the true God from that very God and do not conceive him otherwise than he manifests and declares himself to them.

Source fund.; | related to heart's condition
of knowl. ═══ | wicked heart listens to its vain thought
| true heart listens to ⊙

It is source of this true knowl. which only bel. has
He has it b/c ⊙ revealed Himself by sp- Thus true
knowl. of heart + mind is had.

22

3

What We Must Know of God

Now since the majesty of God in itself goes beyond the capacity of human understanding[14] and cannot be comprehended by it, we must adore its loftiness rather than investigate it, so that we do not remain overwhelmed by so great a splendor. Hence, we must seek and consider God in his works, which, for this reason the Scripture calls representations[15] of the invisible things (Rom. 1:20; Heb. 11:1) because these works represent to us that of the Lord which otherwise we cannot see. Now this does not keep our intellect up in the air through frivolous and vain speculations, but is a thing that we must know and that generates, nourishes, and confirms in us a true and solid piety, that is, faith[16] united with reverential fear.[17] We contemplate, therefore, in this universality of things, the immortality of our God, from which immortality have proceeded the beginning and origin of all things; his power which has created such a great system[18] and now sustains it; his wisdom which has composed and rules[19] with such a distinct order such a great and complex variety of beings and things; his goodness which has been the reason in itself why all these things have been created and now subsist; his justice which manifests itself in a marvelous way in the protection of good people and in the retribution of the bad; his mercy which endures our iniquities with such a great kindliness in order to call us to amendment. Certainly all this should abundantly teach us all of such a[20] God as it is necessary to know, if we in our coarseness were not blind to such a great light. Yet here we

23

sin not only by blindness, for our perversity is such that when it estimates the works of God there is nothing that it does not understand in an evil and perverse sense, so that it turns upside down all the heavenly wisdom which otherwise shines so clearly in those works. It is therefore necessary to come to the word [of God][21] where God is very well described to us through his workings, because in the Scripture these works are estimated not according to the perversity of our judgment, but by the standard of the eternal truth. From God's word, therefore, we learn that our only and eternal God is the spring and fountain of all life, justice, wisdom, virtue, goodness, and clemency. And, as every good without exception comes from him, so also every praise should rightly return to him. And although all these things appear clearly in each part of heaven and earth, yet only then do we at last understand truly that to which they tend, what their value is and at what end we must understand them, when we descend into ourselves and consider in what way the Lord manifests[22] in us his life, wisdom, and power, and exercises toward us his justice, clemency, and goodness.

4
Man

HUMANKIND

At first man was formed in the image and resemblance of God in order that man might admire his Author in the adornments with which he had been nobly vested by God and honor him with proper acknowledgment.[23] But, having trusted such a great excellence of his nature and having forgotten from whom it had come and by whom it subsisted, man strove to raise himself up apart from the Lord.[24] Hence man had to be stripped of all God's gifts of which he was foolishly proud, so that, denuded and deprived of all glory, he might know God whom man, after having been enriched by his liberalities, had dared to despise. As a result, this resemblance to God having been effaced in us, we all who descend from the seed of Adam are born flesh from flesh. For, though we are composed of a soul and a body, yet we feel[25] nothing but the flesh, so that to whatever part of man we turn our eyes, it is impossible to see anything that is not impure, profane, and abominable to God. The intellect[26] of man is indeed blinded, wrapped with infinite errors and always contrary to the wisdom of God; the will, bad and full of corrupt affections, hates nothing more than God's justice; and the bodily strength, incapable of all good deeds, tends furiously toward iniquity.

5

Free Will[27]

The Scripture testifies often that man is a slave of sin. The Scripture means thereby that man's spirit is so alienated from the justice of God that man conceives, covets, and undertakes nothing that is not evil, perverse, iniquitous, and soiled. Because the heart, totally imbued with the poison of sin, can emit nothing but the fruits of sin. Yet one must not infer therefrom that man sins as constrained by violent necessity. For, man sins with the consent of a very prompt and inclined will.[28] But because man, by the corruption of his affections, very strongly keeps hating[29] the whole righteousness of God and, on the other hand, is fervent in all kinds of evil, it is said that he has not the free power of choosing between good and evil—which is called free will.

6

Sin and Death

Sin means in the Scripture both the perversity of human nature, which is the fountain of all vices, and the evil desires which are born from it and the iniquitous transgressions which spring from these evil desires, such as murders, thefts, adulteries, and other things of this kind. Hence, being sinners from our mothers' wombs, we are all born subject to the wrath and retribution of God. And, having grown up, we pile upon ourselves an ever heavier judgment of God. Finally through all our life we tend ever more toward death. For there is no doubt that all iniquity is execrable to the justice of God. What can we expect in the face of God, we miserable ones who are oppressed by such a great load of sins and soiled by an infinite[30] filth, expect a very certain confusion such as his indignation brings? Though it fells man with terror and crushes him with despair, yet this thought is necessary for us in order that, being divested of our own righteousness, having given up faith in our own power, being rejected from all expectation of life, we may learn from the understanding of our poverty, misery, and infamy, to prostrate ourselves before the Lord and, by the acknowledgment of our iniquity, powerlessness, and utter ruin, give him all glory of holiness, might, and deliverance.

7

How We Are Delivered
and Restored to Life[31]

If this knowledge of ourself, which shows us our nothingness, consciously enters into our hearts, an easy access to having the true knowledge of God is made to us. Or rather, God himself has opened to us, as it were, a first door to his kingdom[32] when he has destroyed these two worst pests, which are self-assurance in front of his retribution and false confidence in ourselves. For we begin then to lift our eyes to heaven, those eyes that before were fixed and stopped on earth. And we, who once rested in ourselves, long for the Lord. On the other hand, though our iniquity should deserve something quite different, this merciful Father yet, according to his unspeakable benignity, shows himself voluntarily to us who are thus afflicted and perplexed. And by such means which he knows to be helpful in our weakness, he recalls us from error to the right way, from death to life, from ruin to salvation, from the kingdom of the devil to his own reign.[33] As the Lord has therefore established this first preparation for all those whom he pleases to re-establish as heirs to heavenly life—that is to say, those who distressed by conscience and burdened by the weight of their sins feel themselves stung in the heart and stimulated[34] reverently to fear him—God then first places his Law before us in order that it exercise us in this knowledge.

27

8

The Law of the Lord

In the Law of God a perfect standard of all righteousness is presented to us which with good reason can be called the eternal will of the Lord. For God has completely and clearly comprised in two tables all that which he requires of us. In the first table with a few commandments he prescribes to us what is the service of his majesty which pleases him. In the second table he tells us what are the offices of charity which are due to our neighbor. Let us listen to that Law, therefore, and we shall see afterward what teaching we must draw from it and similarly what fruits we must gather from it.

EXODUS 20

1. *I am the Lord thy God, who has gotten[35] thee out of the land of Egypt, from the house of slavery. Thou shalt not have[36] other[37] gods in my presence.[38]*

The first part of this commandment is like a preface to all the Law. Indeed, when God pronounces himself to be the Lord our God, he declares himself to be he who has the right to command and to whose commandment obedience is due; just as God says by the mouth of his prophet: "If I am Father, where is the love [due to me]? If I am Lord, where is the reverential fear [due to me]?" And likewise he puts into memory his beneficent work, which must convict us of ingratitude if we do not obey his voice. For as by such a benignity he has once delivered[39] the people of Israel from the slavery of Egypt, so likewise he frees all his servants from

28

the perpetual Egypt of believers, that is, from the power of sin.

The prohibition from having other[40] gods means that we must attribute to no other than God all that which is proper to him. And he adds, "In my presence," or sight, meaning that he wishes to be acknowledged as God not only by an external declaration of faith, but in pure truth from the depth of the heart. Now, the following things are proper to God alone and cannot be transferred to another without wresting them away from God:[41] our worshipping him alone, our resting ourself in him with all our reliance and our hope, our acknowledging that whatever good and holy thing comes from him, and our praising him for all goodness and holiness.

2. *Thou shalt not make unto thyself any image nor any resemblance of the things which are in the heaven above[42] or on the earth here below,[43] or in the waters which are below the earth. Thou shalt not nod before such things and not honor them.*

Just as by the former commandment he declares himself to be only one God, so now he announces such as[44] he is and how he must be served and honored. He forbids us, therefore, to counterfeit any resemblance to him, of which thing he gives the reason in Deut., ch. 4:15–18 and in Isa. 40:18–25, that is, because the spirit has nothing similar to the body. Moreover, he prohibits us from honoring any image with religious intention. Hence, let us learn from this commandment that the service and honor of God is spiritual, for, as he is spirit, so he requires to be served and honored in spirit and in truth (John 4:23). He adds then a horrible menace by which he declares how gravely the transgression of this commandment offends him.

For, I am the Lord thy God, mighty, jealous, visiting[45] the iniquity of the fathers on the children until the third and fourth generation in those who hate me, and exercising mercy on a thousand generations[46] toward them who love me and keep my commandments.

29

It is as if God said that he is the only one to whom we must cling; he cannot endure another companion god and will vindicate his majesty and glory if someone will transfer them to images or to another thing; and that not only once,[47] but on fathers, children, and nephews, that is, in all times, just as he will perpetually manifest also his mercy and kindliness[48] toward them who have love for him and keep his Law. And he declares[49] the grandeur of his mercy in this that he extends it to a thousand generations, while he assigns only four generations to his vengeance.

3. *Thou shalt not take in vain the name of the Lord thy God,*[50] *because the Lord will not hold as innocent him who will have taken the name of the Lord his God in vain.*

Here God forbids to abuse, that is, to misuse his sacred and holy name in oaths to confirm vain things or lies, because oaths must not serve our pleasure and enjoyment, but a right and just necessity, when the glory of the Lord must be maintained or when something aiming at edification[51] must be affirmed. God forbids altogether that we stain for any reason his sacred and holy name. He rather wishes that (when we take an oath or for any purpose which we hold from him) we do so reverently and with all the dignity his holiness requires. And since the principal habit of usurping this name is found in the invocation of it, that is, most people abuse his name when they invoke it, let us understand what invocation is here commanded us. Finally, he announces here punishment in order that those who will have profaned the holiness of his name by perjuries and other blasphemies may not think to be able to escape his retribution.

4. *Remember the day of rest in order to sanctify it. Six days thou shalt work and in them do all thy work; the seventh, however, is the rest of the Lord thy God. On it thou shalt not do any work, neither thou, nor thy son, nor thy daughter, nor thy manservant, nor thy maid, nor thy animals, nor the foreigner who is within thy doors. For, in six days God made the heavens, the earth and all the things which are in them, and*

on the seventh day he rested: hence he has blessed the day of rest and has sanctified it.

We see that there were three reasons for giving this commandment: First, with the seventh day of rest the Lord wished to give to the people of Israel an image of spiritual rest, whereby believers must cease from their own works in order to let the Lord work in them.[52] Secondly, he wished that there be an established day in which believers might assemble in order to hear his Law and worship him. Thirdly, he willed that one day of rest be granted to servants and to those who live under the power of others so that they might have a relaxation from their labor. The latter, however, is rather an inferred than a principal reason.

As to the first reason, there is no doubt that it ceased in Christ; because he is the truth by the presence of which all images vanish. He is the reality[53] at whose advent all shadows are abandoned. Hence St. Paul (Col. 2:17) affirms that the sabbath has been a shadow of a reality yet to be.[54] And he declares elsewhere its truth when in the letter to the Romans, ch. 6:8, he teaches us that we are buried with Christ in order that by his death we may die to the corruption of our flesh. And this is not done in one day, but during all the course of our life, until altogether dead in our own selves, we may be filled with the life of God. Hence, superstitious observance of days must remain far from Christians.

The two last reasons, however, must not be numbered among the shadows of old. Rather, they are equally valid for all ages. Hence, though the sabbath is abrogated, it so happens among us that we still convene on certain days in order to hear the word of God, to break the [mystic] bread[55] of the Supper, and to offer public prayers; and, moreover, in order that some relaxation from their toil be given to servants and workingmen. As our human weakness does not allow such assemblies to meet every day, the day observed by the Jews has been taken away (as a good device for elimi-

31

nating superstition) and another day has been destined to this use. This was necessary for securing and maintaining order and peace in the Church.

As the truth therefore was given to the Jews under a figure, so to us on the contrary truth is shown without shadows in order, first of all, that we mediate all our life on a perpetual sabbath from our works so that the Lord may operate in us by his spirit; secondly, in order that we observe the legitimate order of the Church for listening to the word of God, for administering the sacraments, and for public prayers; thirdly, in order that we do not oppress inhumanly with work[56] those who are subject to us.

5. *Honor thy father and thy mother in order that thy days might be lengthened on the land which the Lord thy God will give thee.*

Hereby piety[57] is commanded toward our fathers and mothers and toward those who are likewise constituted above us, such as princes and[58] magistrates; that is to say, we are told to owe them all reverence, obedience, and gratitude, and to render unto them all possible services. For this is the will of the Lord that we return like for like unto those who have put us in this life. It matters little whether or not they are worthy of this honor, for, whatever they are, they have been given to us as father and mother by the Lord, who was willed that we honor them. Incidentally it must be noted that we are not commanded to obey them except in God. As a result, we must not transgress the Law of the Lord to please them, for, if they command us anything against God, in this we must not consider them as father and mother but as strangers who wish to divert us from obedience to our true Father. And this is the first commandment with promise, as St. Paul says to the Ephesians, ch. 6:2, by which the Lord promises the blessing of the present life to the children who shall have served and honored their fathers and mothers with suitable observance. Likewise it declares that a very sure curse is prepared for those who are rebellious and disobedient.

32

6. *Thou shalt not kill.*

Here we are forbidden all violence and injury and in general any offense which might wound the body of our neighbor. For, if we recall that man has been made in the image of God, we must hold our neighbor as holy and sacred, in such a way that he may not be violated without violating also the image of God in him.

7. *Thou shalt not commit fornication and adultery.*[59]

Here the Lord forbids us any kind of lewdness and immodesty.[60] For the Lord has joined man to woman by the law of marriage only; and, as this union[61] is bound by his authority, he has also sanctified it with his blessing. Hence it is clear that any other union outside of marriage is cursed before him. As a result, those who have not the gift of continence (which is certainly rare and not in the power of each) should cure the intemperance of their flesh with the honest remedy of marriage. For, marriage is honorable among all; but God will condemn fornicators and adulterers (Heb. 13:4).

8. *Thou shalt not rob.*

Here we are in general forbidden and prohibited from taking each other's goods. The Lord wishes indeed that all robberies, by which the weak are aggravated and oppressed, be very far from his people, as well as all kinds of fraud, by which the innocence of the simple is deceived. Hence, if we wish to keep our hands pure and innocent from theft, we must abstain no less from all cunning and tricks than from violent ravishings.

9. *Thou shalt not bear false witness against thy neighbor.*

The Lord here forbids all evilspeaking and injuries[62] by which the good name of our brother or sister is hurt, as well as all falsehoods which in any way wound our neighbor. For, if a good name is more precious than any treasure, we suffer no less damage from being robbed of the integrity of our good reputation than from being stripped of our goods. And quite often one has no less profit from carrying off a brother's or sister's goods through false witnessings than by the rapacity of the hands. Hence, just as the former commandment tied the hands, this command ties the tongue.

10. *Thou shalt not covet the house*[63] *of thy neighbor, and thou shalt not desire the wife of thy neighbor nor his manservant, nor his maid, nor his ox, nor his ass, nor any thing belonging to thy neighbor.*

With these words the Lord curbs, as it were, all our cupidities which go beyond the limits set by charity.[64] This commandment indeed forbids conceiving in the heart all that which the other commandments prohibit committing in act against the rule of love.[65] Hence this command condemns hatred, envy, ill will, just as murder was condemned above. Lascivious sentiment and inner impurity of heart are here prohibited just as are acts of fornication. Just as, before, rapacity and cunning were forbidden, so now is avarice. Whereas, before, slander was banned, so now malignity itself is repressed.

We may see how universal the sentence of this commandment is, and how far and wide its extent is. The Lord exacts indeed an extraordinary affection,[66] sovereignly ardent with love,[67] for the brethren—an affection[66] that should not even be perturbed by any evil desire and greed against the good and the profit of the neighbor. This therefore is the sum of this commandment: we must be so affectionate that we are no longer even solicited by any cupidity contrary to the law of love,[65] and ready to render most willingly to each one that which is his. And we must hold toward each as his own that which the duty of our office binds us to render to him.[68]

9

The Summary of the Law

Now our Lord Jesus Christ has clearly enough declared to
us the real purpose of all the commandments of the Law,
when he taught that all the Law is comprised in two articles.[69] The first article is that we should love[70] the Lord our
God with all our heart, with all our soul, and with all
our strength. The second article is that we should love[71] our
neighbor as much as ourselves. And this interpretation, our
Lord has taken from the Law itself. For the first part is found
in Deut. 6:5, and the second is seen in Lev. 19:18.

10

What Comes to Us
from the Law Alone

Behold above, therefore, the standard of a just and holy
life and even a very perfect image of justice or righteousness, so that if someone expresses the Law of God in his life,
he will lack nothing of the perfection required before the
Lord. In order to certify that, God promises to those who
shall have fulfilled the Law not only the grand blessings of
the present life, which are recited in Lev. 26:3–13 and in

Deut. 27:1–14, but also the recompense of eternal life (Lev. 18:5). On the other hand, he pronounces retribution with eternal death against those who shall not have accomplished by deeds that which is commanded in the Law. Moses also, having published the law (Deut. 30:19), took heaven and earth as witnesses that he had proposed to the people good and evil, life and death.

But although the Law shows the way of life, yet we must see what this demonstration can avail us. Certainly if our will be all formed and disposed to obedience toward the divine will, the mere knowledge of the Law would fully suffice for salvation. But as our carnal and corrupt nature altogether wars[72] against the spiritual Law of God and in nothing is mended by the teaching thereof, it results that the very Law (which was given unto salvation if it had found good and capable hearers) becomes on the contrary an occasion of sin and death. For, since we are all convicted of being transgressors of the Law, the more clearly the Law discloses to us the justice of God, the more it uncovers on the other hand our iniquity. And again, as the Law catches us in greater transgression, so it renders us deserving[73] of a heavier judgment of God. And, the promise of eternal life being thus taken away, the curse alone remains for us, which catches us all by means of the Law.

11

The Law Is a Preparation[74] to Come to Christ

The testimony of the Law, however, which convinces us of iniquity and transgression,[75] is not made in order that we should fall into despair, and, having lost courage, stumble into ruin. Certainly the apostle (Rom. 3:19, 20) testifies that every mouth be closed and the entire world be found guilty before God. Yet that very apostle elsewhere (Rom. 11:32) teaches that God has enclosed all under unbelief, not in order to ruin them or let them perish, but, on the contrary, in order that he may exercise mercy on all.

The Lord, therefore, after reminding us (by means of the Law) of our weakness and impurity, comforts us with the assurance of his power and his mercy. And it is in Christ his son that God shows himself to us benevolent and propitious.[76] For, in the Law he appeared only as remunerator of perfect righteousness (of which we are completely destitute) and, on the other hand, as upright and severe judge of sins. But in Christ his face shines full of grace and kindliness even toward miserable and unworthy sinners; for, he gave this admirable example of his infinite love,[77] when he exposed his own son for us, and in him opened to us all the treasure of his clemency and goodness.

12

We Apprehend Christ Through Faith

Just as the merciful Father offers us the Son through the word of the Gospel, so we embrace him through faith and acknowledge him as given to us. It is true that the word of the Gospel calls all to participate in Christ, but a number,[78] blinded and hardened by unbelief, despise such a unique grace. Hence, only believers enjoy Christ; they receive him as sent to them; they do not reject him when he is given, but follow him when he calls them.

37

13

Election and Predestination[79]

Beyond this contrast of attitudes[80] of believers and unbelievers, the great secret of God's counsel must necessarily
be considered. For, the seed of the word of *God* takes root
and brings forth fruit only in those whom the Lord, by his
eternal election, has predestined to be children and heirs of
the heavenly kingdom. To all the others (who by the same
counsel of God are rejected before the foundation of the
world) the clear and evident preaching of truth can be nothing but an odor of death unto death. Now, why does the
Lord use his mercy toward some and exercise the rigor of
his judgment on the others? We have to leave the reason of
this to be known by him alone. For, he, with a certainly
excellent intention,[81] has willed to keep it hidden from us
all. The crudity of our mind could not indeed bear such a
great clarity, nor our smallness comprehend such a great
wisdom. And in fact all those who will attempt to rise to
such a height and will not repress the temerity of their spirit,
shall experience the truth of Solomon's saying (Prov. 25:27)
that he who will investigate the majesty shall be oppressed
by the glory. Only let us have this resolved in ourselves
that the dispensation of the Lord, although hidden from us,
is nevertheless holy and just. For, if he willed to ruin[82] all
mankind, he has the right to do it, and in those whom he
rescues from perdition one can contemplate nothing but his
sovereign goodness. We acknowledge, therefore, the elect to
be recipients of his mercy (as truly they are) and the rejected
to be recipients of his wrath, a wrath, however, which is
nothing but just.

38

Let us take from the lot of both the elect and the others, reasons[83] for extolling his glory. On the other hand, let us not seek (as many do), in order to confirm the certainty of our salvation, to penetrate the very interior of heaven and to investigate what God from his eternity has decided to do with us. That can only worry us with a miserable distress and perturbation. Let us be content, then, with the testimony by which he has sufficiently and amply confirmed to us this certainty. For, as in Christ are elected all those who have been preordained to life before the foundations of the world were laid, so also he is he in whom the pledge of our election is presented to us if we receive him and embrace him through faith. For what do we seek in election except that we be participants in the life eternal? And we have it in Christ, who was the life since the beginning and who is offered[84] as life to us in order that all those who believe in him may not perish but enjoy the life eternal. If, therefore, in possessing Christ through faith we possess in him likewise life, we need no further inquire beyond the eternal counsel of God. For Christ is not only a mirror by which the will of God is presented to us, but he is a pledge by which life is as sealed and confirmed to us.[85]

14

What True Faith Is

One must not imagine[86] that the Christian faith is a bare and mere knowledge of God or an understanding of the Scripture which flutters in the brain without touching the heart, as it is usually the case with the opinion about things which are confirmed by some probable reason. But faith is a

firm and solid confidence of the heart, by means of which
we rest _surely_ in the mercy of God which is promised to us
through the Gospel. For thus the definition of faith must
be taken from the substance of the promise. Faith rests so
much on this foundation that, if the latter be taken away,
faith would collapse at once, or, rather, vanish away.
Hence, when the Lord presents to us his mercy through the
promise of the Gospel, if we certainly and without hesita-
tion trust him who made the promise, we are said to appre-
hend his word through faith. And this definition is not
different from that of the apostle (Heb. 11:1) in which he
teaches that faith is the certainty[87] of the things to be hoped
for and the demonstration of the things not apparent; for he
means a sure and secure[88] possession of the things that God
promises, and an evidence of the things that are not apparent, that is to say, the life eternal. And this we conceive
through confidence in the divine goodness which is offered
to us through the Gospel. Now, since all the promises of
God are gathered together and confirmed in Christ, and are,
so to speak, kept and accomplished in him, it appears without doubt that Christ is the perpetual object of faith. And in
that object, faith contemplates all the riches of the divine
mercy.

15

Faith Is a Gift of God

If we honestly[89] consider within ourselves how much our
thought is blind to the heavenly secrets of God and how
greatly our heart distrusts all things, we shall not doubt that
faith greatly surpasses all the power of our nature and that

faith is a unique and precious gift of God. For, as St. Paul maintains (I Cor. 2:11), if no one can witness the human will, except the spirit of man which is in man, how will man be certain of the divine will? And if the truth of God in us wavers even in things that we see by the eye, how will it be firm and stable where the Lord promises the things that the eye does not see and man's understanding does not comprehend?

Hence there is no doubt[90] that faith is a light of the Holy Spirit through which our understandings are enlightened and our hearts are confirmed in a sure persuasion which is assured[91] that the truth of God is so certain that he can but accomplish that which he has promised through his holy word that he will do. Hence (II Cor. 1:22; Eph. 1:13), the Holy Spirit is called like a guarantee[92] which confirms in our hearts the certainty of the divine truth, and a seal by which our hearts are sealed in the expectation of the day of the Lord. For it is the Spirit indeed who witnesses to our spirit that God is our Father and that similarly we are his children (Rom. 8:16).

16

We Are Justified in Christ Through Faith[93]

Since it is clear that Christ is the perpetual object of faith, we cannot know what we receive through faith except by looking to him. For truly he has been given to us by the Father in order that we may obtain in him life eternal; as he says (John 17:3), life eternal is to know one God the Father and Jesus Christ whom he has sent. And again (John 11:26),

41

he who comes to believe in me shall never die, and if he has died he shall live. Yet, in order that this might be done, it is necessary that we, who are contaminated by stains of sin, be cleansed in him, because nothing defiled shall enter the kingdom of God. Christ, therefore, makes us thus participants in himself in order that we, who are in ourselves sinners, may be, through Christ's righteousness, considered just before the throne of God. And in this manner being stripped of our own righteousness, we are clothed with the righteousness of Christ; and, being unjust by our own deeds, we are justified through the faith of Christ.

For we are said to be justified through faith, not in the sense, however, that we receive within us any righteousness, but because the righteousness of Christ is credited to us, entirely as if it were really ours, while our iniquity is not charged to us, so that one can truly call this righteousness simply the remission of sins. This the apostle evidently declares when he so often compares the righteousness that some imagine they obtain by means of good deeds with the righteousness that comes to us through faith, and teaches that the latter righteousness destroys the former (Rom. 10:3; Phil. 3:9). Now, we shall see in the Symbol[94] in what manner Christ has deserved this righteousness for us and in what[95] this righteousness consists, in which Symbol will indeed be recited in order all the things on which our faith is founded and resting.

17

We Are Sanctified Through Faith in Order to Obey the Law

Just as Christ by means of his righteousness intercedes for us with the Father in order that (he being as our guarantor)[96] we may be considered as righteous, so by making us participants in his spirit, he sanctifies us unto all purity and innocence. For the spirit of the Lord has reposed on Christ without measure—the spirit (I say) of wisdom, of intelligence, of counsel, of strength, of knowledge and reverential fear of the Lord—in order that we all may draw from his fullness and receive grace through[97] the grace that has been given to Christ. As a result, those who boast of having the faith of Christ and are completely destitute of sanctification by his spirit deceive themselves. For the Scripture teaches that Christ has been made for us not only righteousness but also sanctification. Hence, we cannot receive through faith his righteousness without embracing at the same time that sanctification, because the Lord in one same alliance, which he has made with us in Christ, promises that he will be propitious toward our iniquities and will write his Law in our hearts (Jer. 31:33; Heb. 8:10; 10:16).

Observance of the Law, therefore, is not a work that our power can accomplish, but it is a work of a spiritual power. Through this spiritual power it is brought about that our hearts are cleansed from their corruption and are softened to obey unto righteousness. Now the function of the Law is for Christians quite different from what it may be without faith; for, when and where the Lord has engraved in our hearts the love for his righteousness, the external teaching of the Law (which before was only charging us with weakness and transgression) is now a lamp to guide our feet, to the end that we may not deviate from the right path. It is now our wisdom through which we are formed, instructed, and encouraged to all integrity; it is our discipline which does not suffer us to be dissolute through evil licentiousness.

18

Repentance[98] and Regeneration

It is now easy from this to understand why repentance is always joined with the faith of Christ, and why the Lord affirms (John 3:3) that no one can enter the kingdom of heaven except he who has been regenerated. For repentance means conversion, turning over to, whereby, having left the perversity of this world, we return to and in the way of the Lord.[99] Now, as Christ is no minister of sin, so, after having purged us from the stains of sin, he does not clothe us with the participation of his righteousness in order that we may afterward profane with new stains so grand a grace, but in order that, being adopted as children of God, we may consecrate our life course and days to come[100] to the glory of our Father.

The effect of this repentance depends upon our regeneration, which has two aspects,[101] that is to say: the mortification of our flesh, that is, a killing of our inborn corruption;[102] and the spiritual vivification through which man's nature is restored to integrity. We must, therefore, meditate during all our life on the fact that, being dead unto sin and unto our former selves, we may live unto Christ and his righteousness. And since this regeneration is never accomplished as long as we are in the prison of this mortal body, it is necessary that the cure[103] of repentance continues until we die.[104]

19

How the Righteousness Through Good Deeds and the Righteousness Through Faith Fit and Harmonize Together[105]

There is no doubt that good deeds which proceed from such a purity of conscience—as we have just described—are pleasing to God, for, since he recognizes in us[106] his own righteousness, he can but approve and prize it. Yet, we must very carefully guard ourselves that we be not so carried away by the vain confidence in those good deeds that we forget that we are justified by Christ's faith alone.[107] For before God there is no righteousness through works, except that which may correspond to God's own righteousness. As a result, it is not enough that he (who seeks to be considered just through good works) produces certain good deeds, but it is necessary that he obey the Law perfectly.[108] Now, even those who have progressed above all others in the Law of the Lord are still very far from this perfect obedience demanded by the Law.

Moreover, even supposing that the justice of God would content itself with one good work alone,[109] the Lord would yet not find even one[110] good act in his saints for the merit of which he would praise them as just. For although this may seem astonishing, yet it is very true that no work springs from us that is absolutely perfect[111] and is not infected by

45

some stain. Hence, since we are all sinners and have several residues of sins, it is always necessary that we be justified by something outside of ourselves. That is to say, we always need Christ, so that his perfection may cover our imperfection, his purity may wash our impurity, his obedience may efface our iniquity; and finally his righteousness may gratuitously credit us with righteousness. And this, without any consideration at all of our acts, which are not of such value as to stand before the judgment of God. But when our stains, which otherwise might before God contaminate our deeds, are thus covered, the Lord no longer observes anything in these acts except an entire purity and holiness. Hence the Lord honors them with grand titles and praises, for, he calls them just,[112] and promises them a very ample remuneration. Finally, we must thus affirm[113] that the company[114] of Jesus has such a value that because of it we are not only received freely as just, but our very deeds are considered just[115] and are recompensed with an eternal reward.[116]

20

The Symbol of the Faith[117]

It has been said above what we obtain in Christ through faith. Now let us hear what our faith must see and consider in Christ in order to confirm itself. Let us know then that in the Symbol (as it is called) it is explained how the Father has made Christ for us wisdom, redemption, life, righteousness, and sanctification. It can hardly matter which author or authors have composed this summary of faith. It contains no human doctrine. On the contrary[118] it is a collection of very certain testimonies of the Scripture. But in order that the belief we profess in the Father, Son, and Holy Spirit perturb no one, we must first explain it a little. When we name the Father, Son, and Holy Spirit, we do not imagine three Gods. But the Scripture and the very experience of piety show us, in the very simple essence of God,[119] God the Father, his Son, and his Spirit, in such a way that our intellect cannot conceive the Father without comprehending at the same time the Son (in whom brightly shines the vivid image of the Father) and the Spirit (in whom appear the power and virtue of the Father). Let us therefore hold ourselves firm with all the thought of our heart in only one God; yet, nevertheless, let us contemplate the Father with the Son and his Spirit.

I believe in God, the Father almighty,[120] *creator of heaven and earth.*

With these words we are taught not only to believe that God exists, but rather to know what kind of God[121] he is, and to trust that we are of the number of those to whom he promises that he will be their God and whom he receives as his people. All power is attributed to him. It is meant thereby that he administers all things by his providence, rules them by his will, and guides them by his virtue and might.[122] When God is called creator of heaven and earth, it must be understood thereby that he perpetually upholds, maintains, and gives life to all that which he has once created.

And in Jesus Christ, his only Son, our Lord.

Our former teaching that Christ is the true and proper object of our faith appears easily from the fact that all the parts of our salvation are here presented in him. We call him *"Jesus"*[123] (he has been honored with that title through heavenly revelation) because he has been sent to free his people from their sins. For this reason the Scripture affirms

47

(Acts 4:12) that no other name has been given to men in which they shall obtain salvation. The title *"Christ"* signifies that through unction[124] he has been fully endowed[125] with all the graces of the Holy Spirit. These graces are called "oil" in the Scripture, and rightly so, because without them we fall as dry and barren [branches].

Now, through such an unction the Father has constituted him King in order that he subject unto himself all power in heaven and on earth, to the end that we too may become kings in him, having dominion over the devil, sin, death, and hell. Secondly, God has constituted him Priest[126] in order to satisfy the Father for us and to reconcile him through his sacrifice, to the end that in him we too might become priests,[127] offering to the Father prayers, thanksgivings, ourselves, and all things of ours, having him as our intercessor and mediator. Besides all this, Jesus Christ is called Son of God—not, however, like the believers by adoption and grace merely, but truly and by nature. Hence, he is the only and unique[128] Son, to be distinguished from all the others. And he is our Lord, not only according to his divinity, which from all eternity he has had one with the Father, but he is our Lord also according to and in that flesh in which he has been manifested to us. For, as St. Paul says (I Cor. 8:6), there is only one God from whom are all things, and only one Lord Jesus Christ through whom are all things.

Who was conceived of the holy Spirit, born of the virgin Mary.
Here we are told how the Son of God has been made *Jesus* for us, that is to say, Saviour, and *Christ*, that is, anointed as King to keep us, and as Priest to reconcile us with the Father. For he has put on our flesh in order that, being made Son of man, he would make us children of God together with himself; and, having received on himself our poverty, he would transfer his riches to us; having taken on himself our weakness, he would confirm us by his power; having accepted[129] our mortality, he would give us his im-

48

mortality; and being descended to earth, he would raise us to heaven.

He was born of the virgin Mary in order that he would be recognized as the true Son of Abraham and of David, who had been promised in the law and to the prophets, and as true man, in all things similar to us except only in sin, who, having been tempted by all our infirmities, learned to have compassion on them. Yet, he himself has been conceived in the bosom of the virgin through the virtue of the Holy Spirit (marvelous and unspeakable for us), so that he would not be born stained by any carnal corruption, but sanctified by sovereign purity.

Has suffered under Pontius Pilate, was crucified, dead and buried, has descended into hell.[130]

With these words we are taught that he has accomplished our redemption in view of which he was born mortal man, for, the disobedience of man having provoked the wrath of God, he effaced it by his obedience, rendering himself obedient to the Father even to death. And by his death Jesus offered himself to the Father in sacrifice in order to pacify his justice once for all times, to the end that all believers might be eternally sanctified, and eternal satisfaction be accomplished. He has shed his sacred blood for the price of our redemption in order to extinguish the wrath of God inflamed against us and to purge away our iniquity.

But in this redemption there is nothing that is without mystery. He suffered under Pontius Pilate, then judge of the land of Judea, by whose sentence he was condemned as a criminal and malefactor in order that through this condemnation we might be freed and absolved at the consistory[131] of the great Judge. He has been crucified in order to bear on the cross (which was cursed in God's Law) our curse which our sins deserved. He died in order to conquer by his death the death which was against[132] us and in order to swallow that death which otherwise would have swallowed and

49

devoured us all. He has been buried in order that we too (being participants in him by the efficacy of his death) be buried unto sin, being freed from the power of the devil and of death. Concerning the expression that he descended into hell, it means that he was afflicted by God and that he has felt and endured[133] the horrible rigor of his judgment in order to shield us from his wrath and to satisfy his justice for us. Thus he has suffered and borne the penalties due to our iniquity and not to him who was without sin and without stain.

Not that the Father was ever incensed against him, for how could he have been indignant against his Son whom he loved so much, and in whom he was so well pleased? Or, how could he [the Son] have appeased the Father by his intercession if he had provoked God against him? But he is said to have endured the weight of the wrath of God in the sense that, inasmuch as he was struck and afflicted by the hand of God, he felt all the signs of the scorn and retribution of God to the point of being constrained to cry out with anguish, "My God, my God, why hast thou forsaken me?"

On the third day he rose from the dead, he ascended into heaven, is seated at the right hand of God, the Father almighty: from there he will come to judge the living and the dead.

From this resurrection we can have[134] full trust of obtaining victory over the domination of death. For, just as he could not be retained by its pains[135] but rose above all its power, so he has broken all its darts in such a way that they can no longer transfix us mortally. Christ's resurrection is, therefore, first the very certain truth, substance,[136] and foundation of our own resurrection to come; secondly, also of our present vivification by which we are raised to newness of life. By his ascension into heaven, he has opened to us the entrance to the kingdom of heaven, which was once closed to all in Adam; for he has entered heaven in our

50

flesh, as in our name, so that in him we already possess heaven through hope and even sit in celestial places.[137] And he is there with great advantage[138] to us, for, having as eternal priest[139] entered God's sanctuary not made by man's hand, he stands there as perpetual advocate and mediator in our behalf.

As to his being now seated at the right hand of the Father, it means, first, that he is constituted and declared king, master,[140] and lord over all things, in order that by his power he keeps and maintains[141] us so that his reign and his glory is our strength, virtue, and glory against hell. Secondly, it means that he has received all the graces of the Holy Spirit in order to dispense them and enrich therewith believers. Hence, though he has been raised to heaven and the presence of his body has been taken from our sight,[142] yet he does not cease from assisting his faithful ones with his help and power and showing them an evident virtue[143] of his presence. This he has also promised saying, "Behold I am with you until the consummation of the world." Finally, it follows that he will descend from there in a visible form such as he was seen to ascend. This will happen at the last day. He will then appear to all in the incomprehensible majesty of his reign in order to judge the living and the dead. By "living" we mean those whom the last day will surprise and overtake still living. By "dead" we mean those who shall have died before that day. He will then render to all according to their works, as each shall have proved by his deeds to be believer or unbeliever, faithful or unfaithful. And from this comes a unique consolation to us, that is, we do know the judgment to be committed to him whose coming advent can be for us but unto deliverance and salvation.

I believe in[144] *the holy Spirit.*

When we are taught to believe in the Holy Spirit, we are also commanded to expect from him what is said about him[145] in the Scripture. For Christ by virtue of his Spirit

51

works all that which is good, in whatever place that be. By the power of the Spirit, Christ makes, upholds, maintains, and vivifies all things; by it he justifies, sanctifies and purifies, calls and attracts us to himself in order that we may obtain deliverance. Hence, when the Spirit thus dwells in us, it is he who enlightens us with his light in order that we may learn and fully know how great are the riches of the divine goodness which we possess in Christ. It is the Spirit that inflames our hearts with the fire of ardent love[146] for God and for our neighbor. Every day he mortifies and every day consumes more and more the vices of our evil desire or greed,[147] so that, if there are some good deeds in us, these are the fruits and the virtues[148] of his grace; and without the Spirit there is in us nothing but darkness of understanding[149] and perversity of heart.

I believe[150] *the holy Church universal, the communion of saints.*

We have already seen the fountain from which the Church springs. The Church is here set forth to us as object of faith[151] to this end that we may have confidence that all the elect are conjoined through the bond of faith in one Church and society, in one people of God, of which Christ our Lord is the leader[152] and prince and head, as of one body, so that in him they have been elected before the constitution of the world to the end that they may be all assembled in the kingdom of God. This society is catholic, that is to say, universal, because there are not two or three Churches, but all God's elect are united and conjoined in Christ in such a way that just as they depend on one head so they grow as in one body, adhering one to the other, being composed as the members of one same body, being truly made one inasmuch as they live by the same spirit of God in one same faith, hope, and charity, being called to participate in one same inheritance of eternal life. Moreover, the Church is also holy, because all those who are elected by the eternal providence of God to be adopted as members of the Church are all sanctified by the Lord through spiritual regeneration.

The last phrase explains still more clearly what this Church is. That is, the communion of believers is of such a value that if one believer has received any gift from God, all other believers are in some manner made participants in it, although God's dispensation of the gift may be given peculiarly to one person and not to the others. Exactly as the members of one same body through a certain communion[153] participate all among themselves in all the things that they have, and yet each member has by itself particular properties[154] and diverse functions. As it has been said, all the elect are assembled and shaped[155] in one body. Now we believe the[156] holy Church[157] and her communion in such a way that, being assured through firm faith in Christ, we trust to be members of her.[158]

I believe the[156] remission of sins.

On this foundation rests and stands our salvation, because the remission of sins is the way to approach God and the means that retains and preserves us in his kingdom. For all the righteousness of believers is contained in the remission of sins which believers obtain, not through any merit of their own, but through the sole mercy of the Lord. And this takes place when, being oppressed, afflicted, and confused by the consciousness of their sins, they are cast down by the sentiment of God's judgment, are displeased in themselves, and, as under a heavy burden, groan and travail, and through this hatred and confusion of sin they mortify their flesh and all that which is from themselves. But in order to obtain for us gratuitous remission of sins, Christ has himself redeemed and paid[159] with the price of his own blood in which we must seek all purification and all satisfaction for sins. We are therefore taught to believe that through God's liberality, Christ's merit interceding, remission of sins is conceded and grace is done to us who are called and grafted into the body of the Church. And we are taught that no other remission of sins is given anywhere else or by any other means or to others, since outside this Church and communion of saints there is no salvation.

I believe the[160] *resurrection of the flesh,*[161] *the eternal life.*[162] *Amen.*

Here first of all we are taught the expectation of the resurrection to come; that is to say, that it will so happen that the Lord will call back from dust and from corruption to a new life the flesh of those who shall have been consumed by death before the day of the great judgment. And it shall be so through the one same power by which he has resuscitated his Son from the dead. For those who will then be found alive shall pass to new life rather through a sudden transmutation[163] than through natural form of death. Now, as the resurrection will be common to the good and to the bad alike but into different condition, the last part of the statement is added which discerns between our condition and theirs. Our resurrection will be such that, being resuscitated from corruption into incorruption, from mortality into immortality, and being glorified both in body and in soul, the Lord will receive us into a blessedness[164] which will last without end, beyond[165] all quality of mutation and corruption. This will be the true and entire perfection in life, light, and rightness, when we shall be inseparably adhering to the Lord, who, like a fountain that cannot dry up, contains in himself all fullness of life, light, and justice. And this blessedness will be the kingdom of God, filled with all light, joy, power, and felicity.[166] These things are now well beyond men's knowledge and we do not see them except in[167] a mirror and in obscurity until that day shall have come when the Lord will give us to see his glory face to face.

On the contrary, the rejected and the bad[168] who will not have sought and honored God through a true and vivid faith, inasmuch as they shall have part neither in God nor in his kingdom, they shall be thrown with the devils into immortal death and incorruptible corruption, so that, excluded from all joy, power, and all other goods of the celestial kingdom, being condemned to perpetual darkness and eternal torments, they be gnawed by a worm which shall never die and burned by a fire which shall never be quenched.

21

What Hope Is

If Faith (as we have seen) is a sure persuasion of the truth of God which can neither lie nor deceive us and be neither vain nor false,[169] those who have conceived this certainty surely expect likewise that God will accomplish his promises which, according to their conviction,[170] cannot but be true. So that, in sum, Hope is nothing else than the expectation of the things that faith has believed to be truly promised by God. Thus Faith believes God to be truthful: Hope expects that he will show his veracity at the opportune time. Faith believes God to be our Father: Hope expects that he will always act as such toward us. Faith believes the eternal life to be given to us: Hope expects that it shall at some time[171] be revealed. Faith is the foundation on which Hope rests: Hope nourishes and maintains Faith. For, just as no one can expect and hope anything from God, except he who will have first believed his promises, so, on the other hand, it is necessary that our feeble faith (lest it grow weary and fail) be sustained and kept by patient hope and expectation.

22

Prayer

The man rightly instructed in true faith first of all obviously perceives how indigent and denuded of all goods he is and how much he lacks all help of salvation. Hence, if he seeks some succor to assist him in his poverty, he must go out of himself to seek that succor elsewhere. On the other hand, he contemplates the Lord who liberally and out of his good will offers[172] himself in Jesus Christ and in him opens all the heavenly treasures to the end that the whole faith of that man may stop to look at this beloved Son, all his expectation may depend on him, and all his hope may rest and be fixed in him. Nothing therefore remains but that the man seek unto God and ask him in prayer what he has known to exist in God. Otherwise, to know that God is the Lord and distributor of all goods (who invites us to ask of him what we need), to pray to him and to invoke him profit nothing. This would be as if someone, knowing of a treasure hidden in the ground of the earth, abandoned it there through indifference, being unwilling to take the trouble to unearth it.

23

What One Must Consider in Prayer

Prayer is similar to a communication between God and us whereby we expound to him our desires, our joys, our sighs, in a word, all the thoughts of our hearts.[173] Hence, each and every time we invoke the Lord, we must diligently strive to descend in the depth of our heart and from there seek him, and not with the throat or the tongue only. For at times the tongue helps in prayer, either in retaining the spirit more attentive in the meditation of God or in occupying this part of our body (which is especially destined to extol the glory of God) along with the heart to meditate the goodness of God. Yet, the Lord declares through his prophet (Isa. 29:13; Matt. 15:8, 9) what prayer avails without the will,[174] when he has pronounced a very heavy punishment on all those who honor him with their lips, while having their hearts far from him. Moreover,[175] if true prayer must be nothing else than a pure affection of our heart when we should thereby approach God, we must dismiss all thought of our own glory, all fancy of our own dignity and all self-confidence. Thus indeed the prophet (Dan. 9:4–19; Baruch 2:11 ff.) admonishes us to pray, being founded not on our own righteous deeds,[176] but through the great mercies of the Lord, in order that he may answer our prayers out of love for himself, inasmuch as his name is invoked upon us. This knowledge of our misery must not bar our access to God, since prayer has not been instituted in order to raise us arrogantly before God, nor to extol our dignity, but to the end that we confess with sighs our calamities, just as children expound with familiarity their complaints to their fathers. Such a sentiment should rather be like a spur[177] to incite and stimulate us to pray more. Now, there are two things that must marvelously move us to pray. First, the instruction of God by which he commands us to pray. Secondly, the promise whereby he assures us that we shall obtain all that which we will ask.[178] For, those who invoke him, seek him, and depend on him,[179] receive a singular consolation inasmuch as they know that, in doing that, they do a thing pleasing to him. Moreover, being assured of his truth, let them certainly trust that he will answer their prayer. "Ask" (he says: Matt. 7:7) "and it shall be given to you, knock and

57

it will be opened to you; seek and you shall find." And in the psalm (Ps. 50:15): "Call upon me in the day of thy necessity, and I will free thee, and thou wilt glorify me." Here he has comprised or included the two kinds of prayer,[180] which are invocation or request, and thanksgiving. By the former we disclose before God our hearts' desires. By the latter we acknowledge his benefits toward us. We must assiduously use both kinds of prayer, for we are pressed by such poverty and indigence that even the most perfect have sufficient matter to sigh and groan continually, and invoke the Lord with all humility. On the other hand, the liberalities which our Lord by his goodness pours forth upon us are so abundant, and wherever we turn our eyes the miracles of his works appear so great, that we can never lack matter for praise and thanksgiving.

24

Exposition of the Lord's[181] Prayer

Moreover, this merciful Father (besides admonishing and exhorting us to seek him in all necessity, yet seeing still that we do not know enough what we have to ask and what we need) has willed to succor us in this ignorance and has out of his own supplied that which our small capacity lacked. From which kindness we receive a singular consolation inasmuch as it is clear to us that we ask him nothing unreasonable, strange, or out of place, and even not pleasing to him, because [in the *Lord's* Prayer] we pray as it were with or through his own mouth [since it is a *Lord-given* prayer]. This form and rule of praying includes six petitions[182] of which the first three are assigned especially to the glory of

God. This glory alone indeed we must consider in them, without regard for our own profit. The other three are devoted to solicitude for ourselves and to asking the things that pertain to our welfare.[183] Yet the glory of God (which we ask in the first three petitions) carries along with itself our welfare, from the consideration of which we divert our spirit toward that divine glory. On the other hand, it is not legitimate to ask, by the other three petitions, the things useful to us, except in view of the glory of God.

Our Father who art in heaven.

First of all this rule is presented to us: All prayers must be offered to God in the name of Christ, as no prayer in another name can be pleasing to God. For, since we call God our Father, it is certain that we understand beneath it the name of Christ also. Certainly, as there is no man in the world worthy to introduce himself to God and appear in his sight,[184] this good heavenly Father (to free us from this confusion which should have rightly embarrassed us) has given us his Son Jesus to be our mediator and advocate toward him, by whose leading we may boldly approach God, having good confidence that, thanks to this intercessor, nothing which we will ask in his name shall be denied to us, since the Father cannot refuse him anything. And, since the throne of God is not only a throne of majesty but also of grace, we have the boldness to appear frankly in his name before that throne, in order to obtain mercy and find grace when we need it. And, in fact, as we have the ordered law of invoking God and we possess the promise that all those who will call upon him shall be heard, so there is also a special commandment to invoke him in the name of Christ and the promise given of obtaining what we will ask in his name (John 14:13; 16:23).

It is added here that God our Father is in the heavens. His marvelous[185] majesty (which our spirit according to its rudeness cannot otherwise comprehend) is thus signified, inasmuch as there is nothing before our eyes more excellent and full of all majesty than the sky. This phrase "in heaven"[186] is equivalent to saying that God is lofty, mighty, incomprehensible. Now, when we hear that, we must lift on high our thoughts each and every time that God is mentioned, in order not to imagine of him anything carnal and earthly, not to measure him according to our comprehension nor to subordinate his will to our affections.

THE FIRST PETITION
Hallowed[187] *be thy name.*

The name of God is the renown whereby he is celebrated among men for his virtues, as are his wisdom, goodness, might, justice, truth, mercy. We ask therefore that this majesty be sanctified in such virtues of his, not that this majesty may increase or decrease in itself,[188] but that it may be esteemed as holy by all, that is to say, that it may be truly acknowledged and magnified and that (whatever God may do) all his workings may appear glorious as they truly are. So that, if he punishes, he may be held as just; if he forgives, he may be held as merciful; if he accomplishes his promises, he may be held as veracious. In sum, that there may be altogether nothing in which his glory be not as engraved and resplendent, so that praises to him may resound in all spirits and on all tongues.

THE SECOND PETITION
Thy reign[189] *come.*

The reign of God is God guiding and governing his own by his Holy Spirit, in order to manifest in all their works the riches of his goodness and mercy, and, on the contrary,[190] ruining and confounding the reprobate who are unwilling to be subject to his domination and to prostrate their cursed arrogance, in order that it may clearly appear that there is no power that can resist his might. We pray, therefore, that God's reign may come, that is to say, that the Lord may from day to day multiply the number of his faithful believers who celebrate his glory in all works,[191] and that he may continually spread on them more largely the affluence of his graces, whereby he may live and reign in them more and more, until, having perfectly conjoined them to himself, he may fill them wholly. Similarly we ask that from day to day he may through new growths spread his light and enlighten his truth, so that Satan and the lies and the darkness of his reign may be dissipated and abolished. When we pray thus: "May the kingdom[192] of God come," we desire also that it may finally be perfect and accomplished, that is to say, in the revelation of his judgment, in which day he alone will be extolled and will be all things in all people[193] after having gathered and received his own in glory and having demolished and completely overthrown the reign of Satan.

THE THIRD PETITION
Thy will be done as in heaven so also on earth.[194]

By this petition we ask that altogether as it is done in heaven, so also on earth he may rule and guide every thing[195] according to his good will, leading all things to such issue as shall seem good to him, using all his creatures according to his good pleasure, and subjecting all wills to himself. And by asking that, we implicitly renounce all our desires, resigning and promising to the Lord all that which there is of affections in us, praying him to lead things not according to our wish, but as he knows it to be well for us.[196] And even we ask that he not only make vain and of no effect those desires of ours that are contrary to his will, but even more that he may create in us new spirits and new hearts, extinguishing and annihilating ours, so that no movement of greed may arise[197] in us, but only a pure consent to his will. In brief, that we wish nothing from ourselves, but that his Spirit may will in us, through whose inspiration we may learn to love all things pleasing him and to hate and to detest all that which displeases him.

Give us today our daily bread.

By this petition we ask generally all the things that are necessary to the indigence[198] of our body under the elements of this world, not only concerning food and clothing, but all that which God knows to be useful to us, in order that we may eat our bread in peace. With these words (to say it briefly) we recommend ourselves to the providence of the Lord and entrust ourselves to his solicitude, in order that he may nourish us, maintain us, and preserve us. For this good Father does not regard it as unworthy to receive even our bodies in his custody and care, this in order to exercise our trust in him by means of these light and small things, so that we expect from him all our necessities,[199] even to the least crumb of bread and one drop of water. Now, as to our asking our "daily" bread "and for today," it means that we must not wish of it except what is necessary for our necessity and for living day by day. And we must have[200] this trust that, when our Father shall have nourished us today, he will not fail us tomorrow either. Whatever abundance we may have at present, it is fit always to ask our daily bread, acknowledging that all actual possessions are nothing, except in so far as the Lord, by the infusion of his blessing on them, makes them prosper and come to profit, acknowledging also that the actual possessions that are in our hands are not ours except in so far as he dispenses to us their use at every hour, and distributes to us a portion of them. As to our calling this bread "ours," the goodness of God appears to be even greater; for that goodness makes to be ours that which was by no right due to us. Finally, our asking that it be *given* us signifies unto us that it is a simple and free gift of God, from whatever source that bread may come, even though it seems to have been acquired by our industry.

THE FIFTH PETITION
Remit us our debts, as we remit [them] to our debtors.

By these words we ask that grace and remission of our

sins be made unto us, which remission is necessary to all men without exception. And we call our offenses "debts" inasmuch as we owe to God the penalty thereof as the payment of a debt. And we could not meet it in any way if we were not absolved through this remission, which is a gratuitous pardon because of his mercy. We ask that this be done to us as we do it to our debtors, that is to say, as we forgive[201] those by whom we have been wounded, in whatever way, or iniquitously outraged through deeds, or offended through words. The condition, however, is not added as if by forgiving others we deserved the forgiveness of God. But this addition, "As we remit them to our debtors," is simply a sign[202] offered to us by God to confirm us in the certainty that the Lord receives us to mercy as we are certain in our conscience of exercising mercy upon others, if our heart is well purged of all hatred, envy, and revenge. And vice versa, it is a sign that God effaces from the number of his children all those who, being inclined to revenge and unable to forgive, keep enmities rooted in their hearts so that they do not undertake to invoke him as their Father and to ask that the indignation which they nourish against men may not fall upon themselves.

THE SIXTH PETITION

Lead us not into temptation, but free us from the evil one. Amen.

By this petition we do not ask to be exempt from all temptations, by which rather we greatly need to be waked up, stimulated, and agitated for fear[203] that through too long a rest we become too soft and lazy. Besides, the Lord daily tests his elect, instructing them through ignominy, poverty, tribulation, and other kinds of cross.[204] But this is our request, that the Lord along with temptations may equally give the way out, so that we be not conquered and crushed by them; so that being firm and robust by the strength of the Lord, we may constantly stand against all powers combating us. Moreover, our request is that, being received in his safeguard and protection, being sanctified by his spiritual graces, being ruled by his guidance,[205] we may remain invincible above the devil, death, and all the weapons of hell. This is to be freed from the evil one. Now, we must take note how the Lord wishes that our prayers be conformed to the rule of charity. For the Lord does not teach us to ask each one for himself what seems good to him individually without considering our neighbor,[206] but he instructs us to be as solicitous for the good of our brother as for our own good.

25

Perseverance in Prayer

Finally we must well observe this: We must not wish to bind God to certain circumstances, because in this very prayer we are taught not to put on him any law, nor to impose upon him any condition. For, before making any prayer for ourselves, before all things, we ask that his will be done; whereby we submit beforehand our will to his, in order that, as if it were caught and retained by a rein, our will may not presume to wish to range and to submit him under our will. If, having the heart formed in this obedience, we permit ourselves to be governed according to the good pleasure of the divine providence, we shall easily learn to persevere in prayer and wait with patience upon the Lord, while deferring the fulfillment of our desires to the hour set by[207] his will; being assured that, although he does not show himself to us, yet he is always present to us and at his own time will reveal[208] that he did not at all have his ears deaf to our prayers, though they seemed to men to be despised by him. And even if at the end, after long waiting, our mind cannot understand the profit of our praying, and our senses feel no fruit thereof, nevertheless our faith will certify unto us what our mind and sense will not be able to perceive, that is, we shall have obtained [from God][209] all that which was good for us, for he will make us in poverty to possess abundance and in affliction to have consolation. For, even if all things should fail us, yet God will never leave us, inasmuch as he cannot disappoint the expectation and patience of his own. And he alone will be sufficient unto us for all things, inasmuch as he contains in himself all goods, which in the time to come he will fully reveal to us.

26

The Sacraments

The sacraments are instituted [by God][210] to this end that they might be exercises of our faith both before God and before men. And certainly before God they exercise our faith when they confirm it in the truth of God. For, the Lord has presented to us the high and heavenly secrets[211] under earthly things,[212] as he knew it to be good for us in the ignorance of our flesh. Not, indeed, that such qualities be inherent in the nature of the things that are offered to us in the sacrament; but because by the word of the Lord they are marked in this significance. For the promise which is contained in the Word always precedes; the sign[213] is added, which sign confirms and seals that promise and renders it unto us as more certified, as the Lord sees that this is adapted to our crude understanding.[214] For our faith is so small and weak that, if it is not upheld from all sides and sustained by all available means, it is immediately shaken on[215] all sides, agitated, and vacillating. Moreover, the sacraments exercise our faith also toward men when faith issues in public acknowledgment and faith is incited to render praises to the Lord.

27

What the Sacrament Is

The sacrament therefore is an external sign[213] through which the Lord presents and testifies to us his good will toward us in order to sustain us in the weakness of our faith. Or (to speak more briefly and more clearly) the sacrament is a testimony of the grace of God declared by an external sign.[216] The Christian Church uses only two sacraments, which are Baptism and the Lord's Supper.

28

Baptism

Baptism has been given to us by God, to help, first, our faith in him, and, secondly, our profession of faith before[217] men. Faith looks at the promise through which the merciful Father offers us the communication of his Christ, in order that, being clothed with him, we may be participants in all his goods. Yet baptism represents particularly two things:

The first is the purgation which we obtain in the blood of Christ; the second is the mortification of our flesh, which we have had through his death. For the Lord has commanded his own to be baptized in[218] the remission of sins (Matt. 28:19; Acts 2:38). And St. Paul (Eph. 5:26, 27) teaches the Church to be sanctified through her bridegroom, and cleansed through the washing of water unto[218] the word of life. And again (Rom. 6:3–11) St. Paul shows how we are baptized in[218] the death of Christ; that is, we are buried in his death in order that we may walk in newness of life. By these things it is not signified, however, that[219] the water is cause, nor even instrument,[220] of purgation and regeneration, but only that the knowledge of such gifts is received in the sacrament, since we are said to receive, to obtain, and to be appointed to that which we believe to be given by the Lord, be it that then for the first time we know him, or be it that, having known him before, we are more certainly persuaded of it.

Baptism serves likewise as our acknowledgment of faith in the sight of[221] men; because it is a mark[222] by which we publicly declare that we wish to be numbered among the people of God, to the end that we, together with all believers, may serve and honor, with one same religion, one God.[223] Since, therefore, principally through baptism the alliance of the Lord is confirmed with us, we rightly baptize our children, since they are already participants in the eternal covenant through which the Lord promises (Gen. 17:1–14) that he will be God not only of us, but also of our posterity.[224]

29

The Supper of the Lord

The promise that is added to the mystery of the supper declares clearly to what purpose the supper has been instituted, and whither it tends. That is to say, it confirms to us that the body of the Lord has once for all been given in such a way for us, that it is now ours and will be ours perpetually. It confirms that his blood has once been shed in such a way for us that it [is and][225] will be always ours.[226] The signs are the bread and the wine, under which the Lord presents to us the true yet spiritual communication of his body and his blood. This communication is content with the bond of his spirit, and does not require at all a presence of the flesh enclosed under the bread, or of the blood under the wine. For, although Christ, being elevated to heaven, has left his abode on earth in which we are still pilgrims, yet no distance can dissolve his power of nourishing his own with himself.[227] He gives us in the supper an instruction concerning this matter so certain and manifest that without any doubt we must be assured that Christ with all his riches is there presented to us, not less than if he could be put in the presence of our eyes and be touched by our hands; and even he is present with so great a power and efficacy that he not only brings there to our spirits assured confidence of eternal life, but also renders us certain of the immortality of our flesh. For our flesh is already vivified by Christ's immortal flesh, and communicates in some way with his immortality.

Hence, under the bread and wine, the body and blood

are presented, to the end that we may learn not only that they are ours, but that they are for us life and nourishment. So, when we see the bread set apart[228] as the[229] body of Christ, at once we must think of[230] this simile: Just as the bread nourishes, sustains, and preserves the life of our body, so the body of Christ is the food and preservation[231] of our spiritual life. And when the wine is presented to us as a sign of the blood, we must likewise think that such fruits as he brings to the body we receive spiritually from the blood of Christ.

Now, as this mystery is a teaching of God's liberality which is so great toward us, it must also admonish us not to be ungrateful toward such a generous kindliness, but rather to extol it with fitting praises and to celebrate it with thanksgiving. Moreover, it exhorts us to embrace each other mutually by such a unity as that which binds among themselves and conjoins together the members of one same body. For no harsher or more pricking spur could be given to move and to incite among us a mutual charity than when Christ, giving himself to us, invites us not only by his example to give ourselves and to expose ourselves mutually one for the other,[232] but inasmuch as he makes himself common to all, he makes us also all one in himself.

30

The Pastors of the Church and Their Power[233]

Since the Lord has willed that both his word and his sacraments be dispensed through the ministry of men, it is necessary that there be pastors ordained to the churches, pastors who teach the people both in public and in private the pure doctrine, administer the sacraments, and by their good example instruct and form all to holiness and purity of life. Those who despise this discipline and this order do injury not only to men, but to God, and even, as heretics,[234] withdraw from the society of the Church, which in no way can stand together without such a ministry. For what the Lord has once (Matt. 10:40) testified is of no little importance: It is that when the pastors whom he sends are welcomed, he himself is welcomed, and likewise he is rejected when they are rejected. And in order that their ministry be not contemptible, pastors are furnished with a notable mandate: to bind and to loose, having the added promise that whatever things they shall have bound or loosed on earth, are bound or loosed in heaven (Matt. 16:19). And Christ himself in another passage (John 20:23) explains that to bind means[235] to retain sins, and to loose means[235] to remit them. Now, the apostle declares what is the mode of loosing when (Rom. 1:16) he teaches the Gospel to be the power of God unto[236] salvation for each believer.[237] And he tells also the way of binding when he declares (II Cor. 10:4–6) the apostles to have retribution ready against any disobedience. For, the sum of the Gospel is that we are slaves of sin and death, and that we are loosed and freed by the redemption which is in Christ Jesus, while those who do not receive him as redeemer are bound as by new bonds of a graver condemnation.

But let us remember that this power (which in the Scripture is attributed to pastors) is wholly contained in and limited to the ministry of the word. For Christ has not given this power properly to these men[238] but to his word, of which he has made these men[238] ministers. Hence, let pastors boldly dare all things by the word of God, of which they have been constituted dispensators; let them constrain all the power, glory, and haughtiness[239] of the world to make room for and to obey the majesty of that word; let them by means of that word command all from the greatest to the smallest; let them edify the house of Christ; let them demolish the reign of Satan; let them feed the sheep, kill the wolves, instruct and exhort the docile;[240] let them rebuke, reprove, reproach, and convince the rebel—but all through and within the word of God.[241] But if pastors turn away from the word to their dreams and to the inventions of their own minds,[242] already they are no longer to be received as pastors, but being seen to be rather pernicious wolves, they are to be chased away. For Christ has commanded us to listen only to those who teach us that which they have taken from his word.

31

Human Traditions[243]

As we have thus a general thought of St. Paul (that is, that all things in the churches must be done decently and in order) we must not count as human traditions the civic observances by which (as by some bonds of unity) order and honesty stand, and peace and concord are retained in the assemblies of Christians. But rather these observances must be referred to that rule of the apostle, provided that they be not thought necessary for salvation, nor binding consciences through religion, nor related to the service of God, and no piety whatever be put in them. But it is necessary greatly and manfully to resist those rules which, as if they were necessary to serve and to honor God, are made under the name of spiritual laws for binding the consciences, for they not only destroy the liberty which Christ has secured for us, but they obscure also the true religion and they violate the majesty of God, who wishes to reign alone in our consciences through and by means of his word. May this then remain firm and definite: All things are ours provided we belong to Christ (I Cor. 3:21–23); and God is served in vain where are taught doctrines which are merely commandments of men (Matt. 15:1–20).

32

Excommunication[244]

Excommunication is the act whereby those who are manifestly fornicators, adulterers, thieves, homicides, misers, robbers, iniquitous, pernicious, voracious, drunkards, seditious, and prodigal (if they do not amend themselves after having been admonished) are, according to God's commandment, rejected from the company of believers. The Church does not thereby cast them into perpetual ruin and despair. She simply condemns their ways of life and their manners, and, if they do not correct themselves, she makes them already certain of their condemnation. Now, this discipline is necessary among believers because, as the Church is the body of Christ, she must not be polluted and contaminated by such stinking and rotten[245] members who dishonor the head; moreover, in order that the saints be not (as it is usual to happen) corrupted and spoiled by the company of the bad. This discipline is profitable also to the latter themselves that their malice be thereby thus chastised; while tolerance would render them more obstinate, this disciplinary provision confuses them with shame and teaches them to amend themselves.[246] When this result is obtained, the Church with kindliness will receive them again in her communion and in the participation of that union from which they had been excluded. Now, in order that no one despise obstinately the judgment of the Church, or think it to be of little account to have been condemned by the sentence of believers, the Lord testifies that such judgment of the faithful[247] is nothing else than the pronouncement of his sentence, and that what they shall have done on earth is ratified in heaven (Matt. 18:15–18). For they have the word of God, by which they can condemn the perverse, and they have the word by which they can receive in grace those who amend themselves.[248]

33

The Magistrate or Civic Officer[249]

The Lord has not only testified that the status of magistrate or civic officer was approved by him and was pleasing to him, but also he has moreover[250] greatly recommended it to us, having honored its dignity with very honorable titles. For the Lord affirms (Prov. 8:15–16) that the fact that kings rule, that counselors order just things, and that the great[251] of the earth are judges, is a work of his wisdom. And elsewhere (Ps. 82:6–7), he calls them gods, because they do his work. In another place also (Deut. 1:17; II Chron. 19:5–7) they are said to exercise judgment for God, and not for man. And Saint Paul (Rom. 12:8) calls the higher offices[252] gifts of God. But (Rom. 13:1–7) where he undertakes a greater discussion of the matter, he teaches very clearly that their power is ordered[253] by God, and that they are ministers of God for praising those who do good and for accomplishing the retribution of God's wrath on the bad. Hence princes and magistrates must think of Him whom they serve in their office, and do nothing unworthy of ministers and lieutenants of God. All their solicitude must be in this: to keep in true purity the public form of religion, to establish and to guide the life of the people by very good laws, and to procure the welfare and the tranquillity of their subjects,[254] both in public and in private. But this cannot be obtained except through justice and judgment, which two things are to them particularly recommended by the prophet (Jer. 22:1–9). Justice is to safeguard[255] the innocent, to maintain, to keep and to free them; judgment is to resist the audacity of evil men, to repress violence, and to punish misdeeds.

On the other hand, the mutual duty of subjects and citizens is not only to honor and to revere their superiors, but to recommend by prayers to the Lord their salvation and prosperity, to submit willingly to their rule, to obey their laws and constitutions, and not to refuse the charges imposed by them: be they taxes, tolls, tributes, and other contributions, or be they offices, civic commissions, and all the like. So that we must not only render ourselves obedient to superiors who rightly and dutifully administer their higher office,[256] but also it is fit to endure those who tyrannically abuse their power, until, through legitimate order, we be freed from their yoke. For, just as a good prince is a testimony of the divine beneficence for maintaining the salvation of men, so a bad and evil prince is a plague of God for chastising the sins of the people. Yet, let this generally be held as certain that to both[257] the power is given by God, and we cannot resist them without our resisting the ordinance of God.

But from obedience to superiors we must always except one thing: that it does not draw us away from obedience to Him to whose edicts the commands of all kings must yield.[258] The Lord, therefore, is the king of kings, and, once he has opened his sacred mouth, he must be listened to by all and above all. Only after that, we are subject to men who are constituted over us, but not otherwise than in him. If men command us to do something against him, we[259] must do nothing, nor keep any account of such an order. On the contrary, let rather this sentence take place: that it is necessary to obey God rather than men (Acts 4:19).

My people has been captive,
Because it had not had knowledge.

ISAIAH 5:13

How will the young person correct his way?
By taking heed thereto according to thy word.

PSALM 119:9

Notes

FOREWORD TO THE 1992 EDITION

1. Robert Kingdon, ed., *Transition and Revolution: Problems and Issues of European and Reformation History* (Minneapolis: Burgess Publishing Co., 1974), pp. 53–76.

2. J. K. S. Reid, ed., *Calvin: Theological Treatises,* Library of Christian Classics (Philadelphia: Westminster Press, 1954), pp. 48–55.

3. Cf. Joseph P. Christopher, *St. Augustine, The First Catechetical Instruction,* Ancient Christian Writers (Westminster, Md.: Newman Press, 1946); A. F. Mitchell, *Catechisms of the Second Reformation;* Thomas F. Torrance, *The School of Faith* (London: James Clarke & Co., 1959); Samuel William Carruthers, *Three Centuries of the Westminster Shorter Catechism* (Fredericton, New Brunswick: University of New Brunswick, 1957).

4. The critical text of the catechism of 1542, 1545 is in Peter Barth, Wilhelm Niesel, and Dora Scheuner, eds., *Ioannis Calvini Opera Selecta,* vol. 2 (Munich: Chr. Kaiser, 1952).

5. "Farewell Address to Ministers." Calvin wrote the catechism of 1542 in haste and never had the leisure to revise it.

6. Rodolphe Peter, "The Geneva Primer or Calvin's Elementary Catechism," trans. Charles Raynal, in *Calvin Studies V* (Davidson, N.C., 1990). First published in *Revue d'Histoire et de Philosophie Religieuses* 45 (1965): 11–45.

7. *Calvin: Institutes of the Christian Religion,* ed. John T. McNeill, trans. Ford Lewis Battles, Library of Christian Classics (Philadelphia: Westminster Press, 1960), IV. 19. 13 (p. 1461).

8. Sermon 4 on the Letter to Titus.

9. Sermon 121 on Deuteronomy.

10. John Calvin, *Institution of the Christian Religion* (1536), trans. and ed. Ford Lewis Battles (Atlanta: John Knox Press, 1975). See Alexandre Ganoczy, *The Young Calvin,* trans. David Foxgrover and Wade Provo (Philadelphia: Westminster Press, 1987).

HISTORICAL FOREWORD

1. Calvin was already famous in 1536, first, because of his *Prefaces* to the French Bible printed at Neuchâtel in 1535, and then

because of his Latin *Institutio* in six chapters of 1536. The first *Institutio* stated clearly the faith already set forth in print somewhat confusedly by Farel in 1525, and by Lambert of Avignon in 1529. Calvin's *Institutio* of 1536 caused much controversy and objection on the part of Romanists, Anabaptists, and Humanists. Calvin answered his opponents with Biblical thought and quotations from the Church Fathers, which he inserted in his *Institutio*, republished in 1539 in seventeen chapters. He himself translated this *Institutio* of 1539 into French in 1541. Involved in further debates and many controversies, Calvin kept inserting into his book polemical and theological materials against all sorts of opponents. Thus his book grew into the final Latin *Institutes* of 1559, which contained eighty chapters. This final Latin edition was translated into French, mostly by others, in 1560. To understand truly all the pages of this colossal final edition, one first really should understand the position of each opponent of Calvin who caused the additional sections or pages. This task is not easy. Hence, the first editions and early works of Calvin, such as this *Instruction in Faith* (1537), should be more understandable for the pastor and the ordinary modern reader.

2. *"Annis aliquot antequam Lutherana & Caluiniana haeresis oriretur, nulla ferme erat, vt ij testantur, qui etiam tunc viuebant, nulla (inquam) prope erat in iudicijs Ecclesiasticis seueritas, nulla in moribus disciplina, nulla in Sacris literis eruditio, nulla in rebus diuinis reuerentia, nulla propemodum iam erat religio."* Cardinal Bellarmine, *Opera* (Cologne, 1617), Vol. VI, col. 296.

3. French, *reformer*, then written without accent on its first *e*.

4. See the chapter on "John Calvin: Institutes of the Christian Religion" in *Books of Faith and Power*, by John T. McNeill, pp. 29–57. New York and London, 1947.

5. Reformed Christianity had indeed been stated long before Calvin by William Farel in his *Summaire*, "Turin," 1525, and by Lambert of Avignon in his *Somme chrestienne*, Marburg, 1529. These two books, only recently discovered, and not St. Thomas' Works, were sources of Calvin's thought.

6. Several later books of Calvin were dictated to secretaries and translated and edited by assistants. Most of his Commentaries are notes gathered by "certain persons," probably his pupils. The *Prefaces*, however, are by the hand of Calvin himself.

1

7. Latin title of 1538, *Omnes homines ad religionem esse natos*. The first chapters of Farel's 1525 *Summaire* were "I. God" and "II. Man." Paris, 1935 (without pagination).

8. French, *opinion;* Latin of 1538, *sensu.*

9. French, *crainte.* Calvin uses different terms for "fear." See note 203.

10. French, *opinion.*

11. French, *piete;* the original French *Instruction* of 1537 had no accents.

2

12. Latin of 1538, *Quid inter falsam ac veram religionem intersit.*

13. Singular, because for Calvin there is only one false religion (that invented by men) and only one true religion (that revealed by God).

3

14. French, *entendement.*

15. French, *spectacles.*

16. French, *la foy.*

17. French, *crainte.*

18. French, *machine:* "mechanism."

19. Latin of 1538 adds *perpetuo.*

20. French, *quel;* Latin of 1538, *qualis.* See note 121.

21. Latin, *Dei,* added in 1538 Latin version.

22. French, *declaire;* Latin of 1538, *exserat.*

4

23. French, *recognoissance;* Latin of 1538, *gratitudine.*

24. French, *hors du Seigneur.*

25. French, *sentons;* Latin of 1538, *sapimus.*

26. French, *prudence.*

5

27. French, *Du liberal arbitre;* Latin of 1538, *De libera arbitrio.* In 1524 Erasmus had published *De libero arbitrio.* Luther answered by his *De servo arbitrio,* 1525.

28. Latin, *delinquit voluntate propensissima.*

29. French, *a tres fort en hayne.*

6

30. "Infinite," in contrast with God's infinite purity.

7

31. 1538 Latin title, *Quomodo in salutem ac vitam restituamur.*

32. French, *royaume.*

33. French, *regne:* "reign." Dynamic term, somehow different from *royaume* or *royaulme,* "kingdom" or "realm." Throughout this work "reign" indicates that the original French was *regne* and "kingdom" indicates the French *royaume* or *royaulme.*

34. French, *poinctz et picques;* 1538 Latin has simply *excitentur.*

8

35. French, *tyre.*

36. In French simple future: *tu nauras point* (not imperative: *naie point*). Calvin's ethics is an ethics of gratitude to God. In translating the other Commandments, the translator used the term "thou shalt" to indicate that Calvin was employing the simple future rather than the imperative.

37. French, *estrangers.*

38. Literally "before my face."

39. French, *retyre;* 1538 Latin, *vindicavit.*

40. French, *estrangiers.*

41. Latin of 1538 has *sine sacrilegio.*

42. French, *au ciel las sus.*

43. French, *ca bas.* For Calvin there is a contrast between heaven and earth.

44. French, *quel.* See note 121.

45. Calvin, in his commentary on Isa. 10:3, says: "Usually the Lord visits us in two ways: in mercy and in judgment. In both ways indeed he reveals himself and his power to us, both when, out of compassion for us, he rescues us from dangers and when he inflicts retribution upon the impious and the despisers of the Word. Both expressions, or visitations, have the same reason: the Lord does not appear to us except by his workings; hence he gives us some token of his presence so that we do not think that he is absent."

46. Calvin's very generous interpretation of this Bible verse, as meaning "a thousand generations" instead of simply "thousands," is well pointed out in the second chapter of *Books of Faith and Power,* by John T. McNeill, p. 44. New York and London, 1947.

47. 1538 Latin version adds *brevi aut simplici vindicta sed quae in filios, nepotes et pronepotes sit protendenda, qui scilicet paternae impietatis imitatores erunt.*

48. 1538 Latin adds *in longam posteritatem.*

49. French, *declaire;* 1538 Latin, *commendat.*

50. 1538 Latin, *Non usurpabis, nomen domini Dei tui in vanum.*

51. French, *edification;* that is, religious-moral upbuilding.

52. Notice the contrast: works . . . work. . . .

53. French, *corps.*

54. French, *umbre de la chose future.* In Ch. XV of his 1525 *Summaire,* Farel had said, "Ce que ont designe et signifie les figures & commãdementz des ceremonies de la loy couuertemẽt et en umbre, Jesuchrist la enseigne clairement."

55. French, *du pain;* 1538 Latin, *mystici panis.*

56. 1538 Latin omits "with work."

57. French, *piete.* Among early Romans religion was essentially a rereading (*relegere*) with tremendous care (awe) the formulas of divine worship; piety was the feeling of affection and respect for the parents in particular and the family members in general. Among the Greeks, Antigone was the symbol of this piety.

58. 1538 Latin omits "princes and."

59. One expression in French (*Tu ne paillarderas point*) and 1538 Latin (*Non moechaberis*).

60. French, *luxure et impudicite.*

61. French, *societe.*

62. 1537 French, *iniures;* 1538 Latin, *procacitatem conviciosam.*

63. In 1538 Latin version, Calvin puts "the wife" before "the house": *Non concupisces uxorem proximi tui,* etc.

64. French, *charite:* Christian "love"—a gift of the Holy Spirit (I Cor., ch. 13).

65. French, *dilection.*

66. French, *affection.*

67. French, *amour.*

68. This passage of Calvin reflects both the aphorism "*Cuique suum*": "To each his own" of the Roman law and the "Render to all their dues" of Saint Paul, Rom. 13:7.

9

69. 1537 French: *Or nostre Seigneur Jesus Christ nous a assez declaire a quoy tendent tous les commandements de la Loy, quand il a enseigne toute la Loy estre comprinse en deux chappitres.* 1538 Latin: *Quorsum antem universa legis praecepta spectent satis declaravit Christus dominus noster, dum totam legem duobus capitibus comprehensam esse docuit.*

70. French, *aymions;* 1538 Latin, *diligamus.*

71. French, *aymions;* 1538 Latin, *amemus.*

10

72. French, *bataille.* Calvin's Latin version adds *hostiliter.*

73. French, *coupable.*

74. French, *un degre;* 1538 Latin, *gradum.*

75. French, *transgression;* 1538 Latin, *damnatio.*

76. 1538 Latin adds *patrem.*

77. French, *dilection.*

78. French, *plusieurs;* 1538 Latin, *plurimi.*

79. It can be seen in this section and in the one just above that the origins of Calvin's belief in predestination are not philosophical but Biblical and experimental.

80. French, *difference.*

81. French, *tres bonne cause.*

82. French, *perdre.*

83. French, *argument et matiere.*

84. French, *propose;* 1538 Latin, *praepositum.*

85. The parallel passage of the 1539 *Institutio* and 1541 *Institution,* Vol. III, p. 91, says, "Christ is like a mirror in which it is proper to contemplate our election." Notice how Calvin treats of election and predestination not in the former pages about God but in the very midst of the present sections about Christian experience. Cf. the notes of Max Dominicé in 1541 *Institution,* Vol. III, pp. 293–295. Paris, 1938.

86. Or, "think"; French, *estimer.*

87. French, *subsistence.*

88. French, *seure:* "sure"; 1538 Latin, *securam:* "secure."

89. French, *droictement.* Farel (1525 *Summaire,* Ch. VI) had written: "Faith is a grand and unique gift of God through which we are made children of God. It is sentiment, experience, and true knowledge of God our Father."

90. French, *difficulte;* 1538 Latin has *nihil obscurum est.*

91. French, *soit asseuree;* Latin, *statuat.*

92. French, *arre.*

16

93. 1538 Latin title, *In Christo iustificamur per fidem;* French, *Nous sommes iustifiez en Christ par foy.* "We well declare with Saint

Paul that there is no other faith that justifies, except that which is conjoined with charity." 1536 *Institutio* and 1541 *Institution,* Vol. II, p. 261. See notes 64 and 146. We are freely justified on account of Christ through faith—*gratis propter Christum per fidem.* Augsburg Confession (1530), Art. IV. See note 107.

94. French, *Symbole.* By this word Calvin means the "Apostles' Creed."

95. French, *en quoy;* 1538 Latin, *quibus partibus.*

17

96. French, *pleige.*

97. French, *pour.*

18

98. French, *penitence;* 1538 Latin, *poenitentia.* See note 99.

99. We find here the quintessence of the Reformation, which rediscovered the Semitic concept of repentance as preached by the prophets of Israel, John the Baptist, and Jesus. In his Bible marginal note on Matt. 4:17, Martin Luther correctly explained the imperative "repent" as "turn ye," thereby pointing out the Semitic and Prophetic verb *shub* (German, *bekehren*), its corresponding noun being *teshubah* (German, *Bekehrung*). "All the prophets preach *teshubah*," Maimonides had said. All this is clear in Calvin. His first *Institutio* of 1536 already said: "Repentance is a true conversion of our life to following God and the way which he shows us. It proceeds from a right and genuine awe of God (Ezek., ch. 18). It consists in mortification of our flesh [our empirical human nature] . . . and vivification by the Spirit. All the exhortations to repentance by both the prophets and the apostles are to be understood in this sense." *Institution* of 1541, Vol. II, pp. 175, 176. For Farel, "this Repentance is a new creation of heart, when God gives us a new heart, as the Prophet asks, Ps. 50. And thus the works of death die, and those of life come in." Farel, 1525 *Summaire,* Ch. XX, *"De penitence."* Paris, 1935. Farel's and Calvin's words should not be read through later notions. They did not think of faith as chronologically following repentance, but vice versa. For them, God first gives faith. Repentance is a course of life.

100. French, *vie pour ladvenir.*

101. Literally, "consists of two parts."

102. French has the force of the present: *qui est engendree avec nous.*

103. French, *soing . . . nous soit perpetuel jusques a la mort.*

104. Notice how, when Calvin speaks of repentance, the em-

phasis is on the change of life orientation, rather than on the heart's feeling or contrition.

19

105. French, *conviennent ensemble.*

106. French, *en nous;* 1538 Latin, *in illis.*

107. French, *nous sommes justifiez par la seule foy de Christ.* Moderns generally think that it is our own faith that makes us meritorious and praiseworthy in the eyes of God. For Calvin, this notion is heresy; and he warned then already against this deviation. The Reformer held that it is the faith of *Christ* that renders us acceptable to God. We are justified, not by our own faith—*fide,* but through faith—*per fidem.* Faith for him was not an agent, but simply a channel or a bridge. And faith was a gift of God.

108. Literally, "bring a perfect obedience of the law."

109. French, *une seule bonne oeuvre.*

110. French, *une seule.*

111. French, *consommee dentiere perfection.*

112. French, *justice.*

113. French, *arrester.*

114. French, *societe.*

115. French, *justices.*

116. It is clear that Calvin does not oppose good acts in themselves. What he combats is all idea and notion of meritoriousness on men's part. The Christian performs good deeds, not in order to be just in the eyes of God or because it pays, but because in Christ he has been justified by God. Calvin's ethics is an ethics of gratitude to God, full of nobility and distinction. Cf. Max Dominicé's observations in *Institution* of 1541, Vol. II, p. 393.

20

117. French, *Le Simbole de la Foy;* 1538 Latin, *Symbolum fidei.* See notes 94 and 223. Erasmus had published a *Symbolum apostolorum,* translated into French by Berquin, 1523. The *Enchiridion* or *Short Catechism* of Luther had been published in Latin (together with the *Catechismus minor* of John Brenz) at Hagenau in 1529. The editors of the 1541 *Institution* (Vol. I, p. 323) think, however, that Calvin may have read it only later while at Strasbourg, 1538–1541. Luther's *Little Prayer Book* (*Betbuechlein*) 1522, however, had been published in Latin at Strasbourg in 1525 under the title *Precationum aliquot et piarum meditationum enchiridion* and in French at Paris in 1528 under the title *Le livre de vraye et parfaicte oraison.* Calvin's early treatises reflect this elemental explanation of the Ten

Commandments, the Creed, and the Lord's Prayer. See notes in 1541 *Institution*, Vol. II, p. 369; Vol. III, p. 307; Vol. IV, p. 325.

118. French, *ains.*

119. Or, "being of God"; French, *essence de Dieu.*

120. French, *Ie croy en Dieu, la Pere tout puissant* . . . ; 1538 Latin . . . *in unum Deum patrem, omnipotentem.* . . .

121. French, *cognoistre quel est nostre Dieu;* 1538 Latin, *ut esse Deum nostrum cognoscamus.* Calvin never asked what (*quid*) or who (*quis*) God is, for his "virtues" reveal him not as he is in himself but such (*tel*) as he is in relation to us (*qualis erga nos*), and God shows himself nowhere except in the face of Christ, which face can be seen only with the eyes of faith. Cf. *Institutio* of 1539 and *Institution* of 1541 (very end of Ch. I on "The Knowledge of God"), Vol. I, pp. 77–79.

122. French, *puissance;* 1538 Latin, *manu.*

123. I.e., God saves. Cf. *Institutio* of 1536 and *Institution* of 1541, Vol. II, p. 81.

124. "Christ" means "Anointed One." The early works of Calvin (see next paragraph, first line, *Institutio* of 1536, 1539, and *Institution* of 1541, Vol. II, pp. 81–83) emphasized this unction. This idea of spiritual anointing, which mediated the offices of Christ, almost disappeared from the late works of Calvin. The *Institutes* of 1559–1560 present Christ's offices of Prophet, King, and Priest rather abruptly, without clear connection with this charismatic unction.

125. French, *arrouse;* literally, "showered."

126. French, *Sacrificateur* (capital *S*). Luther's treatise *Unum Christum mediatorem* had been translated into French and published at Geneva in 1528. Cf. note in 1541 *Institution*, Vol. II, p. 381.

127. French, *sacrificateurs* (small *s*).

128. French, *seul et unique.*

129. French, *ayant receu.*

130. French, *aux enfers.* In the classics they were simply the abode of the dead.

131. French, *consistoire:* "ecclesiastical court"; 1538 Latin, *tribunal.*

132. French, *estoit contraire;* 1538 Latin, *imminebat.*

133. Latin version of 1538 has *ac divini indicii horrorem severitatemque sensisse, ut irae Dei intercederet.*

134. French, *prendre;* literally, "take."

135. French, *doleurs.*

136. French, *substance;* 1538 Latin, *hypostasis.*

137. French, *aux lieux celestes;* 1538 Latin has simply *inter coelestes.*

138. French, *bien.*

139. French, *selon loffice de sacrificateur eternel.*

140. French, *maistre;* 1538 Latin, *arbiter.*

141. French, *maintiene;* 1538 Latin, *moderetur.*

142. French, *de devant nos yeulx,* literally, "from before our eyes."

143. Or, "manifest power"; French, *vertu manifeste.*

144. French, *au.*

145. Literally, "what is attributed to him in the Scripture."

146. French, *charite.* "Charity is greater than faith, because it is more fruitful, because it is more comprehensive, because it serves for more things, and because it will last forever, while faith and its offices are only for the time of earthly life." *J. Calvino, Institución de la religión cristiana* [1536] *traducción del latin por J. Terán con una introdución por B. Foster Stockwell,* p. 109 (toward the end of Ch. II). Buenos Aires, 1936.

147. French, *concupiscence.*

148. Or, "powers."

149. 1538 Latin has *nostrae sine ipso dotes mentis sunt tenebrae,* etc.

150. Calvin purposely omits "in." The 1536 *Institutio* and 1541 *Institution,* Vol. II, p. 120, insist: *Croyre l'Eglise, et nompas l'Eglise.* Calvin explains: "We believe *in* God inasmuch as our heart sets itself on him as the truthful One, and our confidence reposes *in* him. This expression [*in*] would not fit the Church, nor the remission of sins and the resurrection of the flesh."

151. French, *est ici proposee a croire.*

152. French, *conducteur.*

153. French, *communite.*

154. French, *proprietez;* 1538 Latin, *dotes.*

155. French, *formez;* 1538 Latin, *compacti.*

156. Calvin purposely omits "in." See note 150.

157. 1538 Latin has *sanctam esse ecclesiam.*

158. Calvin did possess the idea that the Church is "the body of Christ and the complement of Christ" here on earth, a continuation of his mission in time and space. Cf. section 32 and Calvin's exposition of Eph. 1:20. The unity of the Church does not rest on earthly organization but only in the invisible Christ. The holiness of the Church does not depend on the character of her members but on the Holy Spirit. Hence, as such the Church is the object of faith, and outside of her there is no salvation (cf. end of next para-

graph). Calvin's idea of the Church is therefore supernational, antisectarian, and very lofty.

159. French, *rachaptee et poyee.*

160. Calvin writes so purposely. Cf. note 150.

161. "Which thing is not only difficult to believe, but utterly unbelievable, if we wish to estimate it according to human reason." *Institutio* of 1539 and *Institution* of 1541, Vol. II, p. 161.

162. Calvin's thought may seem strange to moderns, but for him resurrection precedes life. He writes in his commentary on the Fourth Gospel, ch. 11:25: "First resurrection then life: restoration from death to life comes before the state of [true or eternal] life. The whole mankind is plunged into death. Hence no one shall partake of life, unless one be first resurrected from the dead." Karl Barth takes the word "eternal" as meaning "belonging to the aeon or world to come" when he explains the Symbol of the Apostles according to Calvin. Cf. Karl Barth, *La confession de Foi de l'Eglise— Explication du Symbole des Apôtres d'après le catéchisme* [1545] *de Calvin,* p. 97. Neuchâtel and Paris, 1943.

163. French, *immutation.*

164. French, *beatitude.*

165. French, *hors de.*

166. French, *rempli de toute clarte, joye, vertu et felicite.*

167. French, *par;* literally, "through."

168. French, *les reprouvez et meschans.*

21

169. French, *vaine ou faulsee;* Latin of 1538, *irrita.*

170. French, *opinion.*

171. French, *quelque fois;* 1538 Latin, *aliquando.*

22

172. French, *se offre;* 1538 Latin, *exhibentem.*

23

173. Farel had very beautifully said, "Prayer is an ardent speaking with God." *Summaire,* Ch. XXIV. This book of Farel, 1525, was the first printed French Protestant exposition of the Christian faith.

174. French, *volunte;* 1538 Latin, *animo.*

175. 1537 French, *oultre.* The 1536 *Institutio* had *prima,* "first of all." Cf. note in 1541 *Institution,* Vol. II, p. 309.

176. French, *justices.*

177. 1538 Latin adds *et stimuli.*

178. 1536 *Institutio* parallel passage: "Neither the merit nor the

particular dignity of prayer obtains the things requested. All the hope of prayer rests and depends on the promise of the Lord." *Institution* of 1541, Vol. III, p. 147.

179. In French, one verb, *requierent,* which means both "to seek" (from Latin *requirere,* from *re* and *quaerere* to seek) and "to depend for success upon."

180. 1538 Latin adds *breviter sed eleganter.*

24

181. French, *dominicale.* In 1519 Luther had published in German a treatise translated into Latin since 1520: *Explanatio dominicae orationis.* See also note 117 above. In 1525, Berquin had translated, from Erasmus' paraphrases of the Gospels of Matthew and Luke, an extract dealing with the Lord's Prayer. Bucer had explained the Lord's Prayer in his *Enarrationum in ev. Matthaci . . . libri duo,* 1527. In 1533 Matthew Malingre composed in six stanzas his *Chanson de l'Oraison dominicale.* Cf. notes in 1541 *Institution,* Vol. III, pp. 307, 308.

182. Among the Reformers, Bucer was the first, 1527, to distinguish six petitions (instead of seven) in the Lord's Prayer.

183. Literally, "good"; French, *bien.*

184. Literally, "before his face."

185. French, *merveilleuse;* 1538 Latin, *inenarrabilis.*

186. French, *cieux.* It is perfectly clear here that "heaven" for Calvin is not a local or a spatial expression.

187. French, *sanctifie.*

188. The Latin version of 1538 has *non in Deo ipso cui apud se nihil accedere potest.* However, years later in his *Psychopannychia* (which we know now to have been published at Strasbourg in 1542) Calvin returns to the expressions of the 1537 *Instruction in Faith: Neque enim aliter regnare olim in se Deus potest, quam regnavit ab initio: cujus majestati, nihil accedere aut decedere potest. Sed regnum ejus dicitur, quod omnibus manifestabitur. . . . Regnat igitur Deus jam nunc in electis suis, quos agit Spiritu suo. Regnat & contra diabolum, peccatum & mortem, dum jubet e tenebris lucem splendescere, qua confundantur error & mendacium . . . Sed tunc regnum ejus adveniet, quum implebitur. Implebitur antem, quum plane manifestabit gloriam majestatis suae electis suis ad salutem: reprobis ad confusionem.* Calvin, *Opera Omnia,* Vol. VIII (Amsterdam, 1667), pp. 348, 349.

189. French, *regne:* "reign." Dynamic term, differing somehow from *royaume* or *royaulme,* "realm" or "kingdom." Cf. note 33.

190. So Calvin writes. He means that God's Reign has two antithetic aspects: one positive (guiding and ruling his own by his Holy

Spirit) and one negative (confounding and ruining those who refuse his domination).

191. French, *en toutes oeuvres;* 1538 Latin, *modis omnibus.*

192. French, *royaume.* Cf. notes 33 and 189.

193. French, *tous:* "all people."

194. So the French: *comme au ciel, aussi en la terre.*

195. French, *tout.*

196. 1538 Latin has *ut ipse prospexerit ac decrevit.*

197. French, *sesleve;* 1538 Latin, *sentiatur.*

198. French, *lindigence;* 1538 Latin, *usus.*

199. 1538 Latin, *omnia.*

200. Literally, "having."

201. French, *pardonnons;* 1538 Latin, *parcimus.*

202. To make it perfectly clear that our forgiving others does not bind at all God to forgive us, Bucer had said, 1527, "*Non conditio sed similitudo hic significatur:* not a condition but a simile is here meant." Calvin, following Bucer, said, "*Non conditio sed signum hic significatur:* not a condition [put on God] but a sign [for men] is meant here." Cf. 1541 *Institution,* Vol. III, p. 315. In other words, according to Bucer and Calvin, our forgiving others does not force God to forgive us. But our not forgiving others shuts us off from God's free forgiveness. Jesus already strove to make this point clear, Matt. 18:23–35.

203. French, *paour,* which, as the reader can see, is a different term from *crainte,* or reverential fear of the Lord. Cf. note 9.

204. French, *croix*—probably singular since the cross once carried by Christ and now by believers is the same cross.

205. French, *estans gouvernez par sa conduite;* 1538 Latin, more powerfully, *eius protectione muniti.*

206. Singular. Christian love or caring is here focused on the single, definite neighbor, not spread sentimentally over anonymous masses. Cf. notes 64 and 146.

25

207. Literally, "of."

208. Or, "make clear"; French, *declarera.*

209. Calvin, in parallel passage of 1541 *Institution,* Vol. III, p. 197. In 1519, Luther had published *Tessaradecas consolatoria pro laborantibus et oneratis,* translated into French, 1528, under the title *Consolation chrestienne contre les afflictions de ce monde et scrupules de conscience.*

26

210. Calvin often and section 28, first line. Ch. XVIII of Farel's 1525 *Summaire* was on the sacraments.

211. French, *secrets;* Latin, usually, *arcana*—term to be distinguished from mystery.

212. French, *charnelles;* literally, "carnal."

213. French, *signe.* See note 223.

214. French, *il convient a la capacite de notre rudesse.*

215. French, *en;* literally, "in."

216. French, *signe.* See note 223.

217. Literally, "toward"; French, *envers;* 1538 Latin, *apud.*

218. French, *en;* literally, "in."

219. French, *par*—evidently a misprint for *que.*

220. French, *instrument;* 1538 Latin, *efficaciam.*

221. Literally, "toward."

222. French, *marque.* The parallel passage of 1541 *Institution,* Vol. III, p. 223, has *marque et enseigne.*

223. With reference to the sacraments, Calvin's own terms are very exact and crystal-clear. As a rule, he does not use, like moderns, the term "symbol." Calvin uses the word "Symbol" to indicate the "Apostolic Creed." See sections 16 and 20. Speaking of sacraments, Calvin uses these words: "sign" (French, *signe*), expressing God's benevolence; "mark" (French, *marque*), of his favor; seal (French, *sceau*), confirming God's favor or promise; "mark and badge" (French, *marque et enseigne*), by which believers publicly declare their faith before men (French, *méreau;* Latin, *tessera,* a kind of identity card given to members of corporations and guilds). Each Reformed church had once its *méreau* (Latin, *tessera*), which the elders gave to the members who desired to commune. It corresponds to the "Communion token" known in the Presbyterian church. This subtle distinction of different ideas and hence of words somehow escaped certain interpreters of Calvin. Therefore, they often mistranslated these very different terms by the word "symbol" (not used by Calvin with reference to the sacraments), thereby introducing into the modern world confused and erroneous notions about Calvin's sacramentarian ideas which were truly distinct and accurate. If Calvin should return and survey the situation, he would likely say what he wrote in 1538: "We always arrive too late for repairing such evils once they have broken out . . . and

infected numerous minds. . . . A remedy for it is very difficult; for, it is much harder to get out of a man's mind false opinions than to make them enter therein." Calvin's Preamble to his Latin version of this *Instruction in Faith*, found in Vol. V, cols. 317 ff., of his *Opera* in the *Corpus Reformatorum*.

224. François Lambert of Avignon, in his *Somme chrestienne*, Marburg, 1529 [only one copy of it exists and is in the Library of French Protestantism], Ch. XLVII, had written about Baptism:

"Just as under the law circumcision was the sign of the people of God, so after its time and the revelation of Jesus Christ, Baptism is the external sign of those who publicly acknowledge his holy name.

"Besides, it signifies that just as he died and was raised, so those who belong to him must die to the flesh and to the world, and be raised and renewed in spirit all the days of their lives. Rom., ch. 6.

"And as under the law children received the sign of circumcision, so under the Gospel it is well done to give children the sign of Baptism, and to pray God for them and on them." Given in 1541 *Institution*, Vol. III, p. 321.

29

225. In the parallel passage of his *Institutio* of 1536 and 1539, Calvin inserts "is and." 1541 *Institution*, Vol. IV, p. 7.

226. In the parallel passage of 1541 *Institution*, Vol. IV, p. 9, Calvin underscores "given *for you* . . . shed *for you*."

227. 1538 Latin adds *ac efficiat ut loco absentes tamen praesentissima communicatione fruantur*.

228. French, *sanctifie*.

229. French, *au*; 1538 Latin, *in*.

230. Literally, "conceive."

231. French, *protection*.

232. Singular, which has great force. Ch. XLVIII of Lambert's *Somme chrestienne* was devoted to "The Table of the Lord": "At the holy table of our Lord . . . we receive his true body and blood. We are unwilling, however, to debate superstitiously the manner of his presence. Rather, we simply believe the truth of his worthy word. . . . By receiving this holy sacrament, we testify that we, with the other faithful believers, are members of Jesus Christ, participants of one spirit, and living thereby in one mystic body. He who with such faith receives it . . . has salvation; otherwise he receives his judgment and condemnation." Given in 1541 *Institution*, Vol. IV, pp. 299, 300.

233. Farel had devoted Chs. XXXIII–XXXVI of his 1525 *Summaire* to the pastorate.

234. French, *comme heretiques;* 1538 Latin, *factiose.*

235. Literally, "it is."

236. French, *a.*

237. French, *a chascun croyant.*

238. Literally, "the men," i.e., the men whom Christ sends (see above).

239. French, *haultesse;* whence the English "haughtiness."

240. Docile, easy to teach and willing to obey, from Latin *doceo,* "I teach."

241. It should be clear from this passage that early Protestantism was a rebirth of Israel's Prophetism within the Roman Church of the sixteenth century. Cf. Ernest Renan, *Histoire du peuple d'Israël,* Vol. II, p. 487, Paris, n.d., and Paolo E. Santangelo, *Lutero,* Milan, 1932.

242. French, *testes,* "heads."

243. Cf. Farel's 1525 *Summaire,* Ch. XIV, about the doctrine and tradition of men.

244. This section greatly reflects Ch. XXXII of Farel's 1525 *Summaire*—"De excômuniement."

245. French, *punais et pourriz;* 1538 Latin has one word, *foetidis.*

246. Literally, "by this being confused with shame they learn to amend themselves."

247. French, *fideles.*

248. Calvin in Geneva wanted existing laws (similar to those of Bern and other cities) to be enforced. The reason for this disciplinary rigor, Calvin himself indicated in the dedication (to the Syndics and City Council of Geneva) of his exposition of the Fourth Gospel in 1553. As the Romanists said that all morals in Geneva and among Protestants were dissolved, Calvin wanted to show to the world by making Geneva an example of living Christianity that as a matter of fact it was not so. He there writes: "God by his grace has given us back uncorrupt purity of teaching, religion in its primitive state, a simple worship of God, and a genuine ministration of the sacraments, as they were delivered to us by Christ. But . . . our enemies, in order to excite against us unfounded dislike among the inexperienced, raise a hateful outcry that we have dissolved all

discipline. Their calumny is abundantly refuted . . . by this single fact, that in Geneva we have no contest more severe than about . . . our excessive severity. But since you Syndics and Senators are the best witnesses for myself and for my colleagues, that we are not more rigid and severe than . . . duty . . . compels us to be, as we freely submit to the decision of your consciences respecting us: so, . . . you will easily perceive at a glance the singularly ridiculous impudence of our enemies on this subject."

33

249. French, *Du magistrat;* Latin, *De magistratu.* Farel had devoted the long Ch. XXXVII of his 1525 *Summaire* to the sword and power of justice and corporeal superiority. F. Lambert of Avignon's Ch. XXVIII of the 1529 *Somme chrestienne* read as follows: "Though we are freed through Jesus Christ, we yet owe submission to all according to God, and especially to kings, princes and lords placed above our heads by the divine providence (Ps. 65). It is well known that their estate is from God for vengeance on the bad, and for honor and help to the good; that tributes, tolls, and other such things must be paid to them, whether they be good or bad, if that which they command is not evil (Matt. 22; Rom. 13; I Pet. 2)." Given in 1541 *Institution,* Vol. IV, p. 338.

250. French, *aussi . . . davantage.*

251. French, *magnifiques.*

252. French, *les superioritez;* 1538 Latin, *praefecturas.*

253. French, *est ordonnance.*

254. French, *leurs subiectz;* Latin, *suae ditionis.*

255. French, more powerfully, *prendre en sauvegarde.*

256. French, *superiorite;* 1538 Latin, *imperium.*

257. French, *tant aux uns que aux autres.*

258. French, *cedent.*

259. Literally, "one."

WWW.LYCOS.COM
Xu Classics
WWW.YAHOO.COM